# Readings and Activit[ies]

## with Answer Key

D0354996

## HOLT
# CALL TO
# FREEDOM

### Beginnings to 1877

## HOLT, RINEHART AND WINSTON
### A Harcourt Education Company

Austin · New York · Orlando · Atlanta · San Francisco · Boston · Dallas · Toronto · London

Cover: Christie's Images

Copyright © by Holt, Rinehart and Winston

All rights reserved. No part of this publication may be reproduced or transmitted in any form or by any means, electronic or mechanical, including photocopy, recording, or any information storage and retrieval system, without permission in writing from the publisher.

Teachers using CALL TO FREEDOM may photocopy complete pages in sufficient quantities for classroom use only and not for resale.

Printed in the United States of America

ISBN 0-03-053474-7

2 3 4 5 6 7 8 9   085   04  03 02

# ★ READINGS ★

## The World before the Opening of the Atlantic

★ ★ ★ ★ ★ ★ ★ ★ ★ ★ ★ ★ ★ ★ ★ ★ ★ ★ ★ ★ ★ ★ ★ ★

## PRIMARY SOURCE READING

# Iroquois Creation Legend

*Archaeologists believe that the ancestors of the Iroquois arrived in the Northeast sometime between 1700 and 700 B.C. By about A.D. 1000, the Seneca, Cayuga, Onondaga, Oneida, and Mohawk—the five tribes that would eventually form the Iroquois League—were well established throughout the region. Like most American Indian cultures, the Iroquois created myths describing how the earth and their people came to be. These creation legends were passed down in the oral tradition, told by one person to another. Creation legends often concentrate on values, events, materials, or natural resources that are important to the particular culture. As you read the selection, consider how the myth reflects Iroquois culture.*

### THE COUNCIL TREE

In the faraway days of this floating island there grew one stately tree that branched beyond the range of vision. Perpetually laden with fruits and blossoms, the air was fragrant with its perfume, and the people gathered to its shade where councils were held.

One day the Great Ruler said to his people: "We will make a new place where another people may grow. Under our council tree is a great cloud sea which calls for our help. It is lonesome. It knows no rest and calls for light. We will talk to it. The roots of our council tree point to it and will show the way."

Having commanded that the tree be uprooted, the Great Ruler peered into the depths where the roots had guided, and summoning Ata-en-sic, who was with child, bade her look down. Ata-en-sic saw nothing, but the Great Ruler knew that the sea voice was calling, and bidding her carry its life, wrapped around her a great ray of light and sent her down to the cloud sea.

### HAH-NU-NAH, THE TURTLE

Dazzled by the descending light enveloping Ata-en-sic, there was great consternation [alarm] among the animals and birds inhabiting the cloud sea, and they counseled in alarm.

"If it falls, it may destroy us," they cried.

"Where can it rest?" asked the Duck.

"Only the *oeh-da* (earth) can hold it," said the Beaver, "the *oeh-da* which lies at the bottom of our waters, and I will bring it." The Beaver went down but never returned. Then the Duck ventured, but soon its dead body floated to the surface.

HRW material copyrighted under notice appearing earlier in this work.

Many of the divers had tried and failed when the Muskrat, knowing the way, volunteered to obtain it and soon returned bearing a small portion in his paw. "But it is heavy," said he, "and will grow fast. Who will bear it?"

The Turtle was willing, and the *oeh-da* was placed on his hard shell.

Having received a resting place for the light, the water birds, guided by its glow, flew upward, and receiving the woman on their widespread wings, bore her down to the Turtle's back.

And Hah-nu-nah, the Turtle, became the Earth Bearer. When he stirs, the seas rise in great waves, and when restless and violent, earthquakes yawn and devour.

## ATA-EN-SIC, THE SKY WOMAN

The oeh-da grew rapidly and had become an island when Ata-en-sic, hearing voices under her heart, one soft and soothing, the other loud and contentious [argumentative], knew that her mission to people the island was nearing.

To her solitude two lives were coming, one peaceful and patient, the other restless and vicious. The latter, discovering light under his mother's arm, thrust himself through, to contentions [conflict] and strife, the right born entered life for freedom and peace.

These were the Do-ya-da-no, the twin brothers, Spirits of Good and Evil. Foreknowing their powers, each claimed dominion [supreme power], and a struggle between them began, Hah-gweh-di-yu claiming the right to beautify the island, while Hah-gweh-da-ĕt-gäh determined to destroy [it]. Each went his way, and where peace had reigned discord [disagreement] and strife prevailed.

**UNDERSTANDING WHAT YOU READ** After you have finished reading the selection, answer the following questions in the space provided.

**1.** Where did people live before the creation of the world?

_____

_____

**2.** Why, in your opinion, was Ata-en-sic chosen to help the cloud sea?

_____

_____

**3.** What natural elements, plants, or animals are important enough to the Iroquois life to be mentioned specifically in the myth?

_____

_____

HRW material copyrighted under notice appearing earlier in this work.

**4.** Which characters in this legend suggest that the Iroquois believed in a struggle between forces of creation and death?

_____

_____

## ACTIVITY

On a separate sheet of paper, draw or sketch a scene of one of the events mentioned in the Iroquois creation legend. Then write a brief caption that explains the scene you have drawn.

HRW material copyrighted under notice appearing earlier in this work.

Name _____ Class _____ Date _____

## The World before the Opening of the Atlantic

# LITERATURE READING

## *Song of Roland*

*The earliest existing French epic poem is the* Song of Roland, *composed by a man named Turoldus around the year 1100. The poem tells the story of the battle of Roncevaux on the border of Spain and France in the year 778. The Frankish king Charlemagne had been waging a campaign against Muslims in Spain, but he was forced to return to France to deal with trouble at home. As Charlemagne's army was leaving Spain through a narrow pass in the mountains, the rear guard, led by Count Roland, was attacked by an army of about 400,000 Saracens. Refusing to sound his horn to call for help from Charlemagne, Count Roland and his men fought the Saracens. Count Roland and all of the men in his command died. During the centuries between the battle and the time that Turoldus put the story on paper, the legend was told and retold in the oral tradition. As you read the selection, pay attention to how the poem addresses the medieval ideal of chivalry.*

The pagans arm themselves with Saracen hauberks [tunics of chain mail], nearly all have three layers of mail [armor]. They lace their very strong helmets made in Saragossa, put on their steel swords made in Vienna. They have sturdy shields, spears made in Valence, and white, blue, and red ensigns. They set aside the mules and all the palfreys, they mount their war-horses and ride in close order. The day was clear and the sun was shining, every bit of their equipment is glittering bright. They sound a thousand bugles to make a fine impression, the noise is great and the French have heard it. Oliver said: "Companion, sir, I believe we may have a battle with the Saracens on our hands." Roland replies: "May God grant it to us! We must make a stand here for our king: one must suffer hardships for one's lord and endure great heat and great cold, one must also lose hide and hair. Now let each see to it that he employ great blows, so that bad songs not be sung about us! Pagans [non-Christians] are in the wrong and Christians are in the right. I shall never be cited as a bad example. . . ."

Oliver said: "The pagans have a huge army. Our French, it seems to me, are in mighty small number! Comrade Roland, do sound your horn, Charles will hear it and the army will turn back." Roland replies: "I would be behaving like a fool! I would lose my good name in fair France. I shall immediately strike great blows with Durendal [Roland's sword], its blade will be bloody up to the golden hilt. The vile [extremely bad] pagans shall rue the day they came to the pass, I swear to you, all are condemned to death. . . ."

Oliver said: "I can't believe there'd be any blame in what I propose. I have seen the Saracens from Spain, the valleys and mountains are covered with them. The hillsides, too, and all the plains. The armies of that foreign people are huge, we have a mighty small company." Roland replies: "My

HRW material copyrighted under notice appearing earlier in this work.

determination is greater because of it. May it not please the Lord God nor his angels that France lose its worth on my account! I'd rather die than be disgraced. The Emperor loves us more when we strike well."

Roland is worthy and Oliver is wise: both have amazing courage. When they are on horseback and armed, they shall not avoid battle even if it means death; both counts are worthy and their words noble. The vile pagans ride on like fury. Oliver said: "Roland, see the first of them coming! They're close to us and Charles is very far away. You did not deign [lower your pride] to sound your oliphant [horn]. Were the King here, we would have suffered no harm. Look up toward the Spanish pass: You can see, the rearguard is to be pitied, the ones who form it can never form another." Roland replies: "Don't say such an outrageous thing! . . . We shall make a stand in this place, the first blow and the first cut will be ours. . . ."

Oliver said: "I don't feel like talking. You did not deign to sound your oliphant, so you see no sign of Charles. He knows nothing about it, the worthy man is not at fault, those who are with him over there are not to be blamed. Now ride with all your might! My lord barons, keep the field! I beseech you in God's name, be completely absorbed in striking blows, in giving and taking! We must not forget Charles's battle cry." As soon as he has spoken, the French cry out. Anyone having heard "Monjoie!" shouted on that occasion would remember true courage. Then they ride, God! at such a furious pace! They dig their spurs in vigorously to go as fast as they can, they go to strike, what else could they do? And the Saracens were not afraid of them; see now the Franks and pagans joining battle.

------------------------------------------------------------------

Excerpt (retitled "Legends of Chivalry") by Turoldus from *The Song of Roland: An Analytical Edition*, translated by Gerald J. Brault. Copyright © 1978 by The Pennsylvania State University. Reprinted by permission of *The Pennsylvania State University Press*.

**UNDERSTANDING WHAT YOU READ**   After you have finished reading the selection, answer the following questions in the space provided.

**1.** How do the French discover they are going to be attacked? How do they react?

_____

_____

**2.** Why does Oliver think Roland should call for help?

_____

_____

**3.** Why does the author go into such great detail to describe the armor and weapons of the Saracens?

_____

_____

HRW material copyrighted under notice appearing earlier in this work.

**4.** What is the most important concern that Roland has, and how are his reasons a reflection of the code of chivalry?

_____

_____

**5.** Why do the French believe that God is on their side?

_____

_____

## ACTIVITY

Imagine that you are a reporter who is writing a story about the Battle of Roncevaux. Include your understanding of the battle situation, a description of the scene, and quotations from some of the main characters in the battle.

HRW material copyrighted under notice appearing earlier in this work.

## BIOGRAPHY READING

# Christine de Pisan

*In order to understand life in Europe during the Middle Ages, scholars and students look to the history and literature that was written during this time period. One of the earliest female authors of the Middle Ages was Christine de Pisan. Her writing provides insight into what life was like in the French royal court and what everyday life was like for women in medieval France.*

Christine de Pisan was born in Venice, Italy, around 1364. Her father, Tommaso di Benvenuto da Pizzano, worked as an astrologer-physician at the court of King Charles V. He provided Pisan with a formal education, which was unusual for women during this era. At the age of 15, Pisan married Etienne de Castel, a court official. Castel died suddenly in 1390, leaving Pisan to care for their three young children. Because movable type had not yet been invented, all books were copied by hand. To support her family, Pisan became a copyist in the medieval book trade.

While working as a copyist, Pisan began writing on her own. In 1393 she published her first work, *Poêmes de veuvage (Poems of Widowhood)*, which dealt with the loneliness and hardships of being a widow. Her next collection of poems focused on chivalry and courtly love and brought her to the attention of the French royal court, including King Charles VI.

After 1404 Pisan turned her attention to social criticism and philosophy. Her philosophical works, such as *Livre de la mutacion de Fortune (Book of Changes in Fortune)*, established her reputation as a serious scholar. The French king's brother, Philip of Burgundy, was so impressed with *Livre de la mutacion de Fortune* that he hired Pisan to write the king's official biography.

In most of her works, Pisan tried to appeal to her aristocratic readers' sense of justice. She wrote about vice, virtue, and the ideals of knighthood. She also wrote about women, and became famous for her 1405 history of women, *Livre de la cité des dames (Book of the City of Ladies)*. In this work, Pisan argues that women made important contributions to society—an idea that many people did not acknowledge at the time. She also believes that women should receive a solid education.

Although some scholars consider Christine de Pisan to be an early feminist, she did hold many attitudes common to her time. For example, she believed that women should accept traditional roles as wives and mothers. She did not believe that men and women should have equal rights or that women should enter professions that were dominated by men. She believed that women should take pride in their roles and understand the value of their contributions to society.

HRW material copyrighted under notice appearing earlier in this work.

In her later years, Pisan wrote primarily about France and religion. She wrote her last poem, *Ditié de Jehanne d'Arc,* in 1429. It is believed to be the only poem to have been written in French about Joan of Arc before her execution. Pisan eventually moved to a convent, where she died in 1430 at the age of 65.

**UNDERSTANDING WHAT YOU READ**   After you have finished reading the selection, answer the following questions in the space provided.

**1.** Why did Christine de Pisan work as a copyist?

_____

_____

**2.** How did her writing reflect the experiences of her life?

_____

_____

**3.** What did Christine de Pisan say about the roles of women?

_____

_____

**4.** Who was the audience for her poetry, and why was this audience important?

_____

_____

**ACTIVITY**

Imagine that you are Christine de Pisan. You have just been commissioned to write a biography of King Charles VI of France. On a separate sheet of paper, write a letter to a friend explaining why you think you were chosen for this important task.

HRW material copyrighted under notice appearing earlier in this work.

## The Age of Exploration

★ ★ ★ ★ ★ ★ ★ ★ ★ ★ ★ ★ ★ ★ ★ ★ ★ ★ ★ ★ ★ ★ ★ ★

# PRIMARY SOURCE READING

# First Impressions of the New World

*After a two-month voyage across the Atlantic, Christopher Columbus made landfall in the West Indies on October 12, 1492. He spent the next three months exploring a number of islands in the Caribbean Sea. In February 1493, just before he began his homeward voyage, he sent a letter to the secretary of the Spanish treasury detailing his impressions of the land and people. As you read this excerpt of the letter from* Renaissance and Reformation: 1300–1648, *edited by G. R. Elton, note Columbus's observations of the "Indians," as he called them, of the New World.*

Sir,— Believing that you will take pleasure in hearing of the great success which our Lord has granted me in my voyage, I write you this letter, whereby you will learn how in thirty-seven days' time I reached the Indies with the fleet which the most illustrious [outstanding] King and Queen, our sovereigns, gave to me, where I found very many islands thickly peopled, of all which I took possession without resistance for their Highnesses by proclamation made and with the royal standard unfurled. . . . When I reached Juana [Cuba], I followed its coast to the westward, and found it so large that I thought it must be the mainland,—the province of Cathay [China]; and, as I found neither towns nor villages on the sea-coast, but only a few hamlets [small villages], with the inhabitants of which I could not hold a conversation because they all immediately fled, I kept on the same route, thinking that I could not fail to light upon [encounter] some large cities and towns. At length . . . I . . . returned to a certain harbour which I had remarked, and from which I sent two men ashore to ascertain [determine] whether there was any king or large cities in that part. They journeyed for three days and found countless small hamlets with numberless inhabitants, but with nothing like order; they therefore returned. In the meantime I had learned from some other Indians whom I had seized, that this land was certainly an island. . . . The lands are high and there are many very lofty mountains. . . . [The islands] are all most beautiful, of a thousand different shapes, accessible [easy to reach], and covered with trees of a thousand kinds of such great height that they seemed to reach the skies. . . . The nightingale was singing as well as other birds of a thousand different kinds; and that, in November, the month in which I myself was roaming amongst them. There are palm-trees of six or eight kinds, wonderful in their beautiful variety; but this is the case with all the other trees and fruits and grasses; trees, plants, or fruits filled us with admiration. It contains extraordinary pine groves, and very extensive plains. There is also honey, a great variety of birds, and many different kinds of fruits. They have neither iron, nor steel, nor arms, nor are they competent to use them, not that they are not well-formed and of handsome stature, but because they are timid to a surprising degree.

HRW material copyrighted under notice appearing earlier in this work.

On my reaching the Indies, I took by force, in the first island that I discovered, some of these natives that they might learn our language and give me information in regard to what existed in these parts; and it so happened that they soon understood us and we them, either by words or signs, and they have been very serviceable [helpful] to us. They are still with me, and, from repeated conversations that I have had with them, I find that they still believe that I come from heaven. And they were the first to say this wherever I went, and the others ran from house to house and to the neighboring villages, crying with a loud voice: "Come, come, and see the people from heaven!" And thus they all, men as well as women, after their minds were at rest about us, came, both large and small, and brought us something to eat and drink, which they gave us with extraordinary kindness. . . .

They assure me that there is another island larger than [Hispaniola] in which the inhabitants have no hair. It is extremely rich in gold; and I bring with me Indians taken from these different islands, who will testify to all these things. Finally, and speaking only of what has taken place in this voyage . . . their Highnesses may see that I shall give them all the gold they require, if they will give me but a little assistance; spices also, and cotton, as much as their Highnesses shall command to be shipped; and mastic [kind of paste], hitherto found only in Greece . . . ; slaves, as many of these idolators as their Highnesses shall command to be shipped. I think also I have found rhubarb and cinnamon, and I shall find a thousand other valuable things.

---------------------------------------------------------------------------

From *Renaissance and Reformation: 1300–1648*, edited by G. R. Elton.

**UNDERSTANDING WHAT YOU READ**   After you have finished reading the selection, answer the following questions in the space provided.

**1.** Where did Columbus think he had landed when he reached Cuba?

_____

_____

**2.** What were Columbus's impressions of the landscape of Cuba?

_____

_____

**3.** What did the Indians think of Columbus and his men?

_____

_____

HRW material copyrighted under notice appearing earlier in this work.

**4.** What did Columbus plan to take with him on his return trip to Spain?

_____

_____

**5.** Why do you think he planned to take these particular items with him?

_____

_____

## ACTIVITY

On a separate sheet of blank paper, draw a commemorative stamp illustrating the arrival of Columbus in the New World. Include images that you believe are representative of Columbus's experiences. You may wish to search the Internet through the HRW Go site for examples of commemorative stamps.

go.hrw.com
**SA1 Commemorative Stamp**

HRW material copyrighted under notice appearing earlier in this work.

★ ★ ★ ★ ★ ★ ★ ★ ★ ★ ★ ★ ★ ★ ★ ★ ★ ★ ★ ★ ★ ★ ★ ★

## LITERATURE READING

# Marco Polo in China

*In 1271 Marco Polo accompanied his father, Niccolò Polo, and his uncle, Maffeo Polo, on a trip from Venice to China. Marco Polo spent 20 years traveling around China in the service of Kublai Khan. Polo returned to Venice in 1295 and was captured by the Genoese in 1298. While in prison he met a writer known as Rusticiano or Rustichello, who wrote down Polo's descriptions of his travels. As you read the excerpt, think about why Europeans were fascinated by stories like Polo's.*

You may take it for a fact that more precious and costly wares are imported into Khan-balik than into any other city in the world. Let me give you particulars. All the treasures that come from India—precious stones, pearls, and other rarities—are brought here. So too are the choicest and costliest products of Cathay itself and every other province. This is one account of the Great Khan himself, who lives here, and of the lords and ladies and the enormous multitude of hotel-keepers and other residents and of visitors who attend the courts held here by the Khan. That is why the volume and value of the imports and of the internal trade exceed those of any other city in the world. It is a fact that every day more than 1,000 cart-loads of silk enter the city; for much cloth of gold and silk is woven here. . . .

When the Great Khan is holding court, the seating at banquets is arranged as follows. He himself sits at a much higher table than the rest at the northern end of the hall, so that he faces south. . . . On the right, at a somewhat lower level, sit his sons in order of age, . . . and his grandsons and his kinsmen of the imperial lineage [ancestry]. They are so placed that their heads are on a level with the Great Khan's feet. Next to them are seated the other noblemen at other tables lower down again. And the ladies are seated on the same plan. . . . And they all know their appointed place in the lord's plan. . . . Outside the hall the guests at the banquet number more than 40,000. For they include many visitors with costly gifts, men who come from strange countries bringing strange things, and some who have held high office and aspire to [seek] further advancement. . . .

In the midst of the hall where the Great Khan has his table is a very fine piece of furniture of great size and splendour in the form of a square chest, each side being three paces [steps] in length, elaborately carved with figures of animals finely wrought in gold. The inside is hollow and contains a huge golden vessel in the form of a pitcher . . . which is filled with wine. In each corner of the chest is a vessel with the capacity of a firkin [small wooden barrel], one filled with mares' milk, one with camels' milk, and the others with other beverages. On the chest stand all the Khan's vessels in which drink is served to him. . . .

HRW material copyrighted under notice appearing earlier in this work.

HRW material copyrighted under notice appearing earlier in this work.

You must know that all the Tartars celebrate their birthdays as festivals. The Great Khan was born on the twenty-eighth day of the lunar cycle in the month of September. And on this day he holds the greatest feast of the year, excepting only the new year festival of which I will tell you later. On his birthday he dons a magnificent robe of beaten gold. And fully 12,000 barons and knights robe themselves with him in a similar colour and style—not so costly as his, but still of the same colour and style, in cloth of silk and gold, and all with gold belts. These robes are given to them by the Great Khan. . . . And you must know that the Great Khan gives rich robes to these 12,000 barons and knights thirteen times a year, so that they are all dressed in robes like his own and of great value. You can see for yourselves that this is no light matter, and that there is no other prince in the world besides himself who could bear such an expense. . . .

The new year begins with them in February. . . . On this day all the rulers, and all the provinces and regions and realms where men hold land or lordship under his sway, bring him costly gifts of gold and silver and pearls and precious stones and abundance of [much] fine white cloth. . . .

I can also assure you for a fact that on this day the Great Khan receives gifts of more than 100,000 white horses, of great beauty and price. And on this day also there is a procession of his elephants, fully 5,000 in number, all draped in fine cloths embroidered with beasts and birds. . . . They all defile [march in line] in front of the Great Khan and it is the most splendid sight that was ever seen.

---

From "Kublai Khan" from *The Travels of Marco Polo*, translated by Ronald Latham. Copyright © 1958 by Ronald Latham. Reprinted by permission of *Penguin Books Ltd*.

**UNDERSTANDING WHAT YOU READ** After you have finished reading the selection, answer the following questions in the space provided.

**1.** What examples does Marco Polo use to explain the economic power of the Great Khan?

_____

_____

**2.** At the banquets held by the Great Khan, why did the guests sit at different levels?

_____

_____

**3.** Why do you think the Great Khan provided costly gold robes to barons and knights?

_____

_____

**4.** Why might descriptions of travel to distant lands have fascinated Europeans of Marco Polo's time?

_____

_____

## ACTIVITY

Imagine that you are an advice columnist. One of your readers is seeking advice about traveling to China. He or she has been invited to one of the Great Khan's banquets and needs to learn what to expect and how to behave at the banquet. On a separate sheet of paper, write a letter from your reader and the response you would give him or her.

HRW material copyrighted under notice appearing earlier in this work.

## The Age of Exploration

★ ★ ★ ★ ★ ★ ★ ★ ★ ★ ★ ★ ★ ★ ★ ★ ★ ★ ★ ★ ★ ★ ★ ★ ★ ★ ★

# BIOGRAPHY READING

# Cabeza de Vaca

*Columbus's voyages encouraged many explorers to travel to the Americas. One of these explorers was Álvar Núñez Cabeza de Vaca. Cabeza de Vaca is famous for being one of the first Europeans to explore what is now the southwestern United States. After being shipwrecked on the coast, Cabeza de Vaca and his companions wandered through the regions of Texas, New Mexico, and Arizona for eight years. His journal is one of the earliest written accounts of conditions and life in the American southwest.*

Álvar Núñez Cabeza de Vaca was born into a wealthy Spanish family around 1490. He was raised by his grandfather, one of the conquerors and governor of the Canary Islands. In 1511 Cabeza de Vaca joined the Spanish army and served in Italy, Spain, and the Spanish kingdom of Navarre. He joined Pánfilo de Narváez on an expedition to Florida in 1527. After landing in Florida the following year, Narváez divided his forces in two. One force was sent inland to explore, and the other remained with the ships on the coast. When the land forces returned to the coast, they discovered that the ships had already departed for Cuba. The remaining Spaniards built small boats and tried to sail to Mexico, but they became lost and were shipwrecked on the coast of Texas.

Most of the Spaniards died during the winter from cold and exposure. Cabeza de Vaca and a few others were captured and imprisoned by the Karankawa, a tribe of American Indians who lived along the Texas coast. Several years later, Cabeza de Vaca—along with Alonso del Castillo, Andrés Dorantes, and the Moor Estevánico—escaped and began a long journey to Mexico. The four men wandered through Texas, along the Rio Grande, into southern New Mexico, and through Arizona to a Spanish encampment in western Mexico. Throughout this journey, Cabeza de Vaca encountered a variety of Indians, none of whom spoke languages he recognized. As he traveled westward, Cabeza de Vaca developed a reputation among the Indians as a healer and medicine man. He encouraged this belief to protect himself and his companions.

When Cabeza de Vaca and his men finally reached the border of present-day Mexico, he found a series of abandoned and destroyed villages. This borderland area had been raided recently by Spanish Christians who had carried away most of the villagers as slaves. At first, Cabeza de Vaca was pleased to find these Spaniards because they would be able to help him return to Spain. He soon came into conflict with them, however, because they intended to enslave the Indians that had escorted him to Mexico.

Cabeza de Vaca filed a report with the Spanish viceroy in Mexico City and then returned to Spain. In 1540 he became governor of the Río de la Plata

HRW material copyrighted under notice appearing earlier in this work.

region of Brazil. During his four years in Río de la Plata, he traveled 1,000 miles across southern Brazil. In 1544 he was overthrown, and was sent back to Spain the following year. Soon thereafter he was banished from Spain and spent the rest of his career working as a Spanish official in Africa.

**UNDERSTANDING WHAT YOU READ**   After you have finished reading the selection, answer the following questions in the space provided.

**1.** Why did Cabeza de Vaca travel across Texas to Mexico?

_____

_____

**2.** What did the Indians who met Cabeza de Vaca on his journey to Mexico think of him?

_____

_____

**3.** Why did Cabeza de Vaca clash with other Spaniards in Mexico?

_____

_____

**4.** What did Cabeza de Vaca do after he returned to Spain?

_____

_____

## ACTIVITY

Imagine that you are Cabeza de Vaca. On a separate sheet of paper, draw a map of North America and trace the path you and your companions made from Florida to Mexico. Include in your map major rivers, oceans, and seas. You may wish to search the Internet through the HRW Go site to find information about the region.

 go.hrw.com
**SA1 Cabeza de Vaca**

HRW material copyrighted under notice appearing earlier in this work.

**CHAPTER 3**

### New Empires in the Americas

★ ★ ★ ★ ★ ★ ★ ★ ★ ★ ★ ★ ★ ★ ★ ★ ★ ★ ★ ★ ★ ★ ★ ★ ★

## PRIMARY SOURCE READING

# France and the New World

*French explorer Samuel de Champlain made several voyages to the area known as New France. The narrative of his explorations provides insight into French attitudes toward the land they found and the Native Americans they encountered. As you read the following excerpt, pay attention to how Champlain works to maintain good relations with the Algonquian.*

I had a young lad, who had already spent two winters at Quebec, and who was desirous of going with the Algonquians to learn their language. Pont Gravé and I concluded that, if he entertained this desire, it would be better to send him . . . that he might ascertain [determine] the nature of their country, see the great lake, observe the rivers and tribes there, and also explore the mines and objects of special interest in the localities [areas] occupied by these tribes, in order that he might inform us, upon his return, of the facts of the case. We asked him if it was his desire to go, for I did not wish to force him. But he answered the question at once by consenting to the journey with great pleasure.

Going to Captain Yroquet, who was strongly attached to me, I asked him if he would like to take this young boy to his country to spend the winter with him, and bring him back in the spring. He promised to do so, and treat him as his own son, saying that he was greatly pleased with the idea. He communicated the plan to all the Algonquians, who were not greatly pleased with it, from fear that some accident might happen to the boy, which would cause us to make war upon them. This hesitation cooled the desire of Yroquet, who came and told me that all his companions failed to find the plan a good one. . . . I accordingly went on shore, . . . and we sat down for a conference, together with many other savages of age and distinction in their troops. . . . I said that it was not acting like a brother or friend to refuse me what he had promised, and what could result in nothing but good to them; taking the boy would be a means of increasing still more our friendship with them and forming one with their neighbors; . . . and that if they would not take the boy, as Captain Yroquet had promised, I would never have any friendship with them, for they were not children to break their promises in this manner. They then told me that they were satisfied with the arrangement, only they feared that, from change of diet to something worse than he had been accustomed to, some harm might happen to the boy, which would provoke my displeasure. This they said was the only cause of their refusal.

I replied that the boy would be able to adapt himself without difficulty to their manner of living and usual food, and that, if through sickness or the fortunes of war any harm should befall him, this would not interrupt my friendly feelings toward them, and that we were all exposed to accidents,

HRW material copyrighted under notice appearing earlier in this work.

which we must submit to with patience. But I said that if they treated him badly, and if any misfortune happened to him through their fault, I should in truth be displeased. . . .

They said to me: "Since, then, this is your desire, we will take him, and treat him like ourselves. But you shall also take a young man in his place, to go to France. We shall be greatly pleased to hear him report the fine things he shall have seen." I accepted with pleasure the proposition, and took the young man. He belonged to the tribe of the Ochateguins, and was also glad to go with me. This presented an additional motive for treating my boy still better than they might otherwise have done. I fitted him out with what he needed, and we made a mutual promise to meet at the end of June.

---

From *Voyages of Samuel de Champlain, 1604–1618*, edited by W. L. Grant.

### UNDERSTANDING WHAT YOU READ
After you have finished reading the selection, answer the following questions in the space provided.

**1.** Why did Champlain think it was a good idea to send someone to live among the Algonquian?

_____

_____

**2.** Why did the Algonquian object to Champlain's suggestion?

_____

_____

**3.** Why did Champlain agree to take an Ochateguin back to France?

_____

_____

**4.** How might this exchange affect relations between France and the Algonquian?

_____

_____

### ACTIVITY

Imagine that a year has passed, and the young Ochateguin has returned from his time in France. You are a tribal elder who had been assigned the task of finding out what he learned from his experience. On a separate sheet of paper, write five questions that you would ask the young Ochateguin. Then pair up with another student in class, exchange your questions, and answer them as you believe the young Ochateguin would.

HRW material copyrighted under notice appearing earlier in this work.

## New Empires in the Americas

★ ★ ★ ★ ★ ★ ★ ★ ★ ★ ★ ★ ★ ★ ★ ★ ★ ★ ★ ★ ★ ★ ★ ★ ★

### LITERATURE READING

# Through the Eyes of a Spanish Missionary-Explorer

*Friar Junípero Serra (1713–1784) was a scholarly Franciscan missionary who came to California in 1769 with Gaspar de Portolá, the founder of San Diego. The following selection is taken from Friar Serra's journal of his travels in California, which is a lively chronicle of exploration. It is also an analysis for the geography and people of California from the point of view of a western European schooled in the Roman Catholic tradition. Read the selection, and answer the questions that follow.*

[June] 20. We continued our journey which lasted five hours, crossing deep ravines, sometimes with the greatest difficulty, climbing up and down hills, without any intermission [break]. After an hour, from a hilltop we saw the West Coast Sea that we had been so anxious to reach. And at the end of the day's march we camped upon the beach. . . . The place had pasture but no drinking water either for the men or the animals. We identified this place with what is called on the maps and sea charts: La Ensenada de Todos Los Santos.

[June] 21. We pushed on following the direction of the shore from northeast to southwest. . . . After two hours and a half of march, we arrived at the north horn of the said bay, and we pitched camp at a distance of a rifle-shot from the ocean. It is pleasant country, all good land, extending as far as the hills which are not very high. There are plenty of green trees along the river bank, which is dry at present; good and abundant water, sufficient for a town. . . . The countryside is covered with green grass and is able to retain considerable humidity, and it is a place where it rains. As a matter of fact this space is just waiting for a mission; what with the nearness to the ocean, its level stretch of beach and its fine bay, it would be situated [located] wonderfully well to ship in and out produce and commodities of all kinds. . . .

[June] 23. We started from that place to re-enter the line of mountains encircling this end of the bay, and in less than an hour's marching, we found ourselves again on the seashore. We followed it the rest of the way—in all, three hours and a half—all good, level road on hard ground until it meets with a mountain which abuts against the ocean itself. At its foot, in a hollow, is a very green meadow with numerous pools of water, sweet and good. There we halted for the night. At this spot there is a large ranchería [group of huts or cottages] of gentiles [non-Christian Native Americans] with whom we visited and were very much delighted: their fine stature, deportment, conversation and gaiety won the hearts of all of us. They loaded us down with fish and abalones [large California shellfish]; they went out in their little canoes to fish especially for us; they put on their dances for our benefit and insisted we sleep there two nights. Anything we told them in Spanish they

HRW material copyrighted under notice appearing earlier in this work.

repeated to us very distinctly. . . . This place does not seem fit for any purpose other than what it now serves: a ranchería; and so we called it La Ranchería de San Juan. The women are very decently dressed, but the men are naked like the rest of them. They carry on their shoulders a quiver [container for arrows] as you see in pictures. On their heads they wear a kind of circlet made of otter or other fine fur. Their hair is cut just like a wig and plastered with white clay, all done very neatly. May God make their souls attractive too! Amen.

[June] 24. . . . After Mass there was an exchange of trinkets between the soldiers and gentiles, bartering pieces of white cloth—to which they are very partial—for basketfuls of fresh fish. In this they showed themselves to be real businessmen: if the piece of cloth was small, the amount of fish in exchange was less—with no arguing allowed. But when the piece was larger, they doubled the quantity of fish. We parted from our good hosts and started on our day's march. . . . After an hour's going we came in sight of the ocean again. It seemed near, but was at quite a distance should we have tried to get to it. We crossed a valley full of trees—alders and live oaks—but without water. Finally after crossing a number of ranges of hills, we arrived at an immense valley, with wonderful pasture, and at its extremities plenty of trees; there was a fair-sized river and lake of clear water. This place, it would appear, could support another good mission; we called it San Juan Bautista.

--------

From *Writings of Junípero Serra*, Vol. 1, ed. Antonine Tibesar, O.F.M. Copyright © 1955 by Academy of American Franciscan History. Reprinted by permission of *Academy of American Franciscan History, Father James McManamon*.

**UNDERSTANDING WHAT YOU READ**   After you have finished reading the selection, answer the following questions in the space provided.

**1.** What features of the California landscape does Serra observe and describe?

_____

_____

**2.** What qualities does Serra look for in the places he visits? Why?

_____

_____

**3.** How did the Native Americans act toward the Spaniards? Why do you think they treated them in this way?

_____

_____

HRW material copyrighted under notice appearing earlier in this work.

**4.** What does Serra seem to think about the Native Americans' business transactions?

_____

_____

**5.** Explain what Serra means by the comment "May God make their souls attractive too!"

_____

_____

## ACTIVITY

Imagine that you are an American Indian living on a mission founded by Junípero Serra. Create a sketch of the mission grounds with labels indicating the locations of important buildings. You may wish to search the Internet through the HRW Go site for more information.

 go.hrw.com
**SA1 San Juan Capistrano**

HRW material copyrighted under notice appearing earlier in this work.

**CHAPTER 3**

## New Empires in the Americas

★ ★ ★ ★ ★ ★ ★ ★ ★ ★ ★ ★ ★ ★ ★ ★ ★ ★ ★ ★ ★ ★ ★ ★

## BIOGRAPHY READING

# Martin Luther

*As the power and influence of the Catholic church expanded, some people began to question certain church practices. One of these people was Martin Luther. Luther believed, for example, that some church practices contradicted the teachings of the Bible. Although the Catholic Church strongly criticized Luther, his questioning led to the beginning of the Protestant Reformation.*

Martin Luther was born in the mining town of Eisleben, Germany, in 1483, to Margaretha and Hans Luther. He received his basic education at schools in Magdeburg and Eisenach. Later he studied at the University of Erfurt, where he earned a bachelor's degree in 1501 and a master's degree. Luther entered an Augustinian monastery and four years later in 1507, the priesthood. He moved to Wittenberg, where he became a professor of theology in 1512.

Luther believed faith alone could guarantee salvation and that no amount of good works could wipe away sins. This belief brought Luther into conflict with the Catholic Church. On a mission to Rome in 1510, he discovered that the pope was raising money to build St. Peter's Basilica by allowing the sale of indulgences, or forgiveness for sins in exchange for a donation.

In 1517 Luther drew up a list of 95 theses, or statements, outlining his opposition to indulgences and other church practices. Luther nailed these theses to the church door at Wittenberg Castle. His action inspired many other Germans to demand reform in the church. This began what would come to be known as the Protestant Reformation.

At first, Pope Leo X ignored Luther. By 1518, however, Luther had created such a stir that the pope summoned him to Rome. Luther did not go. Instead, he continued his attack on the corruption of the Catholic Church.

The pope issued a papal bull, or official decree, against Luther. Luther responded by burning the decree in front of a group of doctors, students, and citizens of Wittenberg. The pope excommunicated him, or expelled him from the church, for his actions. Later, the Holy Roman Emperor Charles V called Luther to the city of Worms to renounce his teachings before the Imperial Diet, a council of rulers in the Holy Roman Empire. When Luther refused to retract his teachings, the Diet proclaimed him an outlaw. Luther's patron and protector, Frederick of Saxony, quickly helped Luther escape to the safety of his castle in southeastern Germany.

While at Wartburg, Luther developed his doctrine of the "priesthood of all believers." This doctrine held that all believers could have a direct relationship with God—in other words, believers did not need the guidance of a priest or other religious authority. This doctrine won him the support of many German princes, who resented the power and wealth of the church.

HRW material copyrighted under notice appearing earlier in this work.

After he left Wartburg, Luther continued writing and taking part in philosophical discussions with other leading thinkers of the day. As he continued to write and debate, Luther reworked his ideas into the doctrine of a reformed church. This doctrine held that only faith made people righteous, that the Bible was the only source of faith, that each person can interpret the Bible without a priest, and that priests should be allowed to marry.

**UNDERSTANDING WHAT YOU READ**   After you have finished reading the selection, answer the following questions in the space provided.

**1.** How did Luther think people could achieve salvation?

_____

_____

**2.** Why did Luther's ideas gain support from German princes?

_____

_____

**3.** Why did the pope excommunicate Luther?

_____

_____

**4.** What did the doctrine of the "priesthood of all believers" state?

_____

_____

**ACTIVITY**

Imagine that you are Martin Luther. You plan to participate in a debate among philosophers about reforming the church. On a separate sheet of paper, prepare an outline of the ideas you will be expressing. Keep in mind that other thinkers will disagree with you. Anticipate their counterarguments by preparing a concise list of what these might be, and be ready to argue the merit of your own ideas.

HRW material copyrighted under notice appearing earlier in this work.

**The English Colonies**

★ ★ ★ ★ ★ ★ ★ ★ ★ ★ ★ ★ ★ ★ ★ ★ ★ ★ ★ ★ ★ ★ ★ ★ ★

# PRIMARY SOURCE READING

## Journal of Sarah Kemble Knight

*Everyday life in North America was challenging and full of dangers for English colonists. Although colonists worked hard to carve towns and villages out of the wilderness, it took longer to build roads to connect different communities. Colonists usually traveled on horseback or by wagon, and faced bad weather, raging rivers, wild animals, and the possibility of conflict with American Indians. Sarah Kemble Knight wrote about some of these dangers. In 1704 Mrs. Knight traveled from Boston, Massachusetts to New York City, New York. While on her journey, Mrs. Knight kept a journal that reveals some of the difficulties faced by colonial travelers. As you read the excerpt, consider the living conditions Mrs. Knight experienced during her trip.*

About eight in the morning, I with the post [mail carrier] proceeded [went] forward without observing anything remarkable; and about two, afternoon, arrived at the post's second stage, where the western post met him and exchanged letters. Here, having called for something to eat, the woman brought in a twisted thing like a cable, but something whiter; and laying it on the board, tugged for life to bring it into a capacity to spread; which having with great pains accomplished, she served us a dish of pork and cabbage, I suppose the remains of Dinner. The sauce was of a deep purple, which I thought was boiled in her dye kettle; the bread was Indian and everything on the table service agreeable to these. I, being hungry, got a little down; but my stomach was soon cloyed [unsettled], and what cabbage I swallowed served me for a cud the whole day after.

Having here discharged the ordinary [paid the bill] for self and guide (as I understood was the custom), about three, afternoon, went on with my third guide, who rode very hard . . . Being come to Mr. Havens', I was very civilly received, and courteously entertained, in a clean and comfortable house; and the good woman was very active in helping me off [with] my riding clothes, and then asked what I would eat. I told her I had some chocolate, if she would prepare it; which with the help of some milk, and a little clean brass kettle, she soon effected [made] to my satisfaction.

I then . . . [went] to my apartment, which was a little room parted from the kitchen by a single board partition [room divider]; where, after I had noted the occurrences of the past day, I went to bed, which, though pretty hard, was neat and handsome. . . .

I got up very early, in order to hire somebody to go with me to New Haven, being in great perplexity [anxiety] at the thoughts of proceeding alone; which my most hospitable entertainer observing, himself went, and soon returned with a young gentleman of the town, who he could confide in to go with me; and about eight this morning, with Mr. Joshua Wheeler my

HRW material copyrighted under notice appearing earlier in this work.

new guide, taking leave of this worthy gentleman, we advanced towards Seabrook. The roads all along this way are very bad, encumbered [filled] with rocks and mountainous passages, which were very disagreeable to my tired carcass [body]; But we went on with a moderate pace which made the journey more pleasant. But after about eight miles riding, in going over a bridge under which the river run very swift, my horse stumbled, and very narrowly escaped falling over into the water; which extremely frightened me. But through God's goodness I met with no harm, and mounting again, in about half a mile's riding, come to an ordinary [inn], were well entertained by a woman of about seventy. . . .

From hence [there] we went pretty briskly forward, and arrived at Saybrook ferry about two of the afternoon; and crossing it, we called at an inn to bait [rest] (foreseeing we should not have such another opportunity 'til we come to Killingsworth).

------------------------------------------------------------

From "The Private Journal of a Journey from Boston to New York" from *The Norton Anthology of American Literature*, third edition, Vol. I, 1989.

**UNDERSTANDING WHAT YOU READ**  After you have finished reading the selection, answer the following questions in the space provided.

**1.** Why did the postal carriers meet one another?

_____

_____

**2.** Why do you think Knight preferred to travel with a guide as opposed to traveling alone?

_____

_____

**3.** What were some of the dangers and discomforts that colonial travelers faced on the roads?

_____

_____

**ACTIVITY**

Imagine that you are an English colonist who has to make a long journey. Make a list of things that you will need to arrange for, such as transportation or a guide, and also make a list of items that you will need to bring for the trip.

HRW material copyrighted under notice appearing earlier in this work.

## The English Colonies

★ ★ ★ ★ ★ ★ ★ ★ ★ ★ ★ ★ ★ ★ ★ ★ ★ ★ ★ ★ ★ ★ ★

# LITERATURE READING

# Mary Rowlandson's Captivity

*The English colonists faced difficulties establishing farms, homesteads, and settlements when they first arrived in North America. They also were under the threat of attack from hostile American Indians because the colonists had settled on American Indian land. On June 20, 1675, Metacomet—whom the colonists called Philip—began a series of attacks on colonial settlements that became known as King Philip's War. At the end of the war, hundreds of English houses had been burned, about 600 colonists were dead, and thousands of American Indians had lost their lives. One of the most famous victims of these attacks is Mary Rowlandson. She was taken prisoner and held in captivity for 11 weeks. She was then ransomed and reunited with her husband and surviving children. Rowlandson published a record of her life in captivity in 1682, which became a popular text in both England and the American colonies. As you read the selection, consider the choices made by Rowlandson.*

But to return: the Indians laid hold of us, pulling me one way, and the children another, and said, "Come go along with us"; I told them they would kill me: they answered, if I were willing to go along with them, they would not hurt me.

Oh the doleful [sad] sight that now was to behold . . . this house! . . . Of thirty-seven persons who were in this one house, none escaped either present death, or a bitter captivity, save only one . . . . There were twelve killed, some shot, some stabbed with their spears, some knocked down with their hatchets. . . . It is a solemn sight to see so many Christians lying in their blood . . . yet the Lord by His almighty power preserved [saved] a number of us from death, for there were twenty-four of us taken alive and carried captive.

I had often before this said that if the Indians should come, I should choose rather to be killed by them than taken alive, but when it came to the trial my mind changed; their glittering weapons so daunted my spirit, that I chose rather to go along with those (as I may say it) ravenous [hungry] beasts, than that moment to end my days; and that I may the better declare what happened to me during that grievous [unfortunate] captivity, I shall particularly speak of the several removes [departures] we had up and down the wilderness.

Now away we must go with those barbarous creatures, with our bodies wounded and bleeding, and our hearts no less than our bodies. About a mile we went that night, up upon a hill within sight of the town, where they intended to lodge. . . . Oh the roaring, and singing and dancing, and yelling of those black creatures in the night . . . . And as miserable was the waste that was there made of horses, cattle, sheep, swine, calves, lambs, roasting pigs, and fowl (which they had plundered [stolen] in the town), some roasting, some lying burning, and some boiling to feed our merciless enemies; who

HRW material copyrighted under notice appearing earlier in this work.

were joyful enough, though we were disconsolate [depressed]. All was gone, my husband gone (at least separated from me, he being in the bay; and to add to my grief, the Indians told me they would kill him as he came homeward); my children gone, my relations and friends gone, our house and home and all our comforts—within door and without—all was gone (except my life), and I knew not but the next moment that might go too. . . .

But now, the next morning, I must turn my back upon the town, and travel with them into the vast and desolate [empty] wilderness, I knew not whither [where]. It is not my tongue, or pen, can express the sorrows of my heart, and bitterness of my spirit that I had at this departure: but God was with me in a wonderful manner, carrying me along, and bearing up my spirit, that it did not quite fail.

--------------------------------------------------------

From "A Narrative of the Captivity and Restoration of Mrs. Mary Rowlandson" from *The Norton Anthology of American Literature,* third edition, Vol. I, 1989.

**UNDERSTANDING WHAT YOU READ**   After you have finished reading the selection, answer the following questions in the space provided.

**1.** How many colonists were killed in the attack? How many were captured?

_____

_____

**2.** Why does Rowlandson allow herself to be captured?

_____

_____

**3.** What do Rowlandson's captors do the night after the attack?

_____

_____

**4.** Why, according to Rowlandson, was she able to survive her captivity?

_____

_____

**ACTIVITY**

Imagine that you are an English colonist who has been captured during a raid in King Philip's War and put to work in an American Indian village. Write a brief account of your captivity, including the work you have to do, the structure and activities of the village, and the daily lives of the villagers.

HRW material copyrighted under notice appearing earlier in this work.

# Squanto

*The English colonists who arrived in America found a land of wilderness populated by American Indian tribes. Although some tribes were hostile, many Indians befriended the new settlers and tried to help them learn about living on unfamiliar land and other important survival techniques. One of the American Indians who helped the Pilgrims was a man named Squanto.*

Squanto was born sometime around 1590. He was a member of the Pawtuxet tribe, who lived along the coast of Maine. In 1605 Squanto was probably captured and taken to England by George Weymouth. He returned to America in 1615 with Captain John Smith's expedition to New England. Shortly thereafter, Captain Thomas Hunt kidnapped and sold Squanto and about 30 other Indians into slavery in Spain.

Squanto eventually escaped from slavery and made his way to England. Once there, he worked for John Slany, treasurer of the Newfoundland Company. After traveling to Newfoundland and then back to England, Squanto piloted Captain Thomas Dermer's expedition to New England in 1619. He left the expedition before it reached Cape Cod, Massachusetts, and made his way back to the home of his tribe. When he arrived, he found that his entire tribe was dead, probably victims of smallpox, which had been brought to the Americas by the English.

Squanto went to live with the Wampanoag tribe, who lived about 40 miles from his native home, near present-day Plymouth, Massachusetts. When the Pilgrims arrived in 1620, Squanto befriended them. He was introduced to the Pilgrim leaders by Samoset, an American Indian leader. Squanto soon became a guide, interpreter, and helper to the English colonists. He helped the Pilgrims negotiate a treaty with the Wampanoag tribe and their chief, Massasoit. This treaty of mutual assistance lasted almost 40 years.

Because Squanto did not really have a home or tribe of his own, he spent a great deal of time with the Pilgrims. He taught them how and where to plant their corn and how to find the best places for fishing.

Squanto began to make enemies among the Indians because of his close friendship with the colonists and because he pretended to have the power to spread the smallpox plague. Then, in the spring of 1622, he stated falsely that Massasoit was going to betray the Pilgrims. When the Wampanoag chief learned of this incident, he demanded that Squanto return to the tribe to be punished. Eventually, Squanto made peace with the Wampanoag.

In November 1622, while acting as a guide and interpreter on Governor Bradford's expedition around Cape Cod, Squanto fell ill with a fever. He died at Chatham Harbor on Cape Cod within a few days.

HRW material copyrighted under notice appearing earlier in this work.

**UNDERSTANDING WHAT YOU READ**   After you have finished reading the
selection, answer the following questions in the space provided.

**1.** When was Squanto first taken to England? What happened when he returned to
America in 1615?

_____

_____

**2.** What did Squanto discover when he returned to America with Captain Thomas
Dermer's expedition?

_____

_____

**3.** List three ways that Squanto helped the Pilgrims in the Plymouth Colony.

_____

_____

**4.** Why did Squanto begin to make enemies among the Indians?

_____

_____

## ACTIVITY

Imagine that you are going to make a movie based on the life of Squanto. On
a separate sheet of paper, write down some ideas for the movie title, some
significant scenes that you would include, and what the main theme of the
movie would be.

HRW material copyrighted under notice appearing earlier in this work.

**CHAPTER 5**

## Life in the English Colonies

★ ★ ★ ★ ★ ★ ★ ★ ★ ★ ★ ★ ★ ★ ★ ★ ★ ★ ★ ★ ★

# PRIMARY SOURCE READING

# "Sinners in the Hands of an Angry God"

*Many English colonists migrated to America in part to obtain religious freedom. Consequently, religion played an important role in the daily lives of colonists. Beginning in the 1730s, a spirit of revivalism transformed religious life in the colonies. This period of religious revival is known as the "Great Awakening." One of the most important ministers during this time was Jonathan Edwards. Edwards believed that it was not enough to understand religious ideas. He thought that a true believer had to understand that he or she was at the mercy of a powerful and sometimes unforgiving God. As you read the selection, consider how Edwards emphasizes salvation.*

O sinner! Consider the fearful danger you are in: it is a great furnace of wrath [anger], a wide and bottomless pit, full of the fire of wrath, that you are held over in the hand of that God . . . . You hang by a slender thread, with the flames of divine wrath flashing about it, and ready every moment to singe [scorch] it, and burn it asunder [apart]; and you have no interest in any Mediator [peacemaker], and nothing to lay hold of to save yourself, nothing to keep off the flames of wrath, nothing of your own, nothing that you ever have done, nothing that you can do, to induce [convince] God to spare you one moment. . . .

Consider this, you that are here present that yet remain in an unregenerate [unconverted] state. That God will execute [act out] the fierceness of His anger implies that He will inflict wrath without any pity. When God beholds the . . . extremity [desperation] of your case, and sees your torment to be so vastly disproportioned [unequal] to your strength, and sees how your poor soul is crushed, and sinks down, as it were, into an infinite gloom; He will have no compassion upon you, . . . or in the least lighten His hand; there shall be no moderation or mercy, nor will God then at all stay His rough wind; He will have no regard to your welfare, nor be at all careful . . . should [you] suffer too much in any other sense, than only that you shall not suffer beyond what strict justice requires.

How dreadful is the state of those that are daily and hourly in the danger of this great wrath and infinite misery! But this is the dismal case of every soul in this congregation that has not been born again, however moral and strict, sober and religious, they may otherwise be. Oh that you would consider it, whether you be young or old! There is reason to think that there are many in this congregation now hearing this discourse [talk] that will actually be the subjects of this very misery to all eternity. We know not who they are, or in what seats they sit, or what thoughts they now have. It may be they are now at ease, and hear all these things without much disturbance, and are now

HRW material copyrighted under notice appearing earlier in this work.

flattering themselves that they are not the persons, promising themselves that they shall escape. If they knew that there was one person, and but one, in the whole congregation, that was to be the subject of this misery, what an awful thing would it be to think of! If we knew who it was, what an awful sight would it be to see such a person! How might all the rest of the congregation lift up a lamentable [sad] and bitter cry over him! But, alas! instead of one, how many is it likely will remember this discourse [discussion] in hell? . . .

And now you have an extraordinary opportunity, a day wherein Christ has thrown the door of mercy wide open, and stands in calling and crying with a loud voice to poor sinners; a day wherein many are flocking to Him, and pressing into the kingdom of God. Many are daily coming from the east, west, north and south; many that were very lately in the same miserable condition that you are in are now in a happy state, with their hearts filled with love to Him who has loved them, and washed them from their sins in His own blood, and rejoicing in hope of the glory of God. How awful is it to be left behind at such a day! . . . To see so many rejoicing and singing for joy of heart, while you have cause to mourn for sorrow of heart, and howl for vexation [frustration] of spirit! How can you rest one moment in such a condition?

-----------------------------------------------------------------

From "Personal Narrative" from *The Norton Anthology of American Literature*, third edition, Vol. I, 1989.

## UNDERSTANDING WHAT YOU READ  After you have finished reading the selection, answer the following questions in the space provided.

**1.** What image does Edwards use to describe the condition of sinners?

_____

_____


**2.** What does Edwards say about those people who think they are saved simply because they lead moral and religious lives?

_____

_____


**3.** How does Edwards try to convince his listeners to become saved?

_____

_____


## ACTIVITY

On a separate sheet of paper, create an advertisement that conveys the same message as this sermon. You might choose to draw illustrations, create an advertising slogan, or choose another method to persuade readers.

HRW material copyrighted under notice appearing earlier in this work.

**CHAPTER 5**

## Life in the English Colonies

★ ★ ★ ★ ★ ★ ★ ★ ★ ★ ★ ★ ★ ★ ★ ★ ★ ★ ★ ★ ★ ★ ★ ★

## LITERATURE READING

# Narrative of the Life of Olaudah Equiano

*Olaudah Equiano, the son of an elder in Benin, was enslaved by other Africans at the age of 11. Eventually he was sold to a European slave trader and shipped to Barbados. Equiano was sold several times, until he was permitted to purchase his freedom in 1766. His autobiography was published by London abolitionists in 1789. The selection below describes conditions on board the ship that carried him to Barbados. As you read the excerpt, consider the treatment that enslaved Africans received.*

At last, when the ship we were in, had got in all her cargo, they made ready with many fearful noises, and we were all put under deck, so that we could not see how they managed the vessel. But this disappointment was the least of my sorrow. The stench [very bad smell] of the hold while we were on the coast was so intolerably loathsome [disgusting], that it was dangerous to remain there for any time, and some of us had been permitted to stay on the deck for the fresh air; but now that the whole ship's cargo were confined together, it became absolutely pestilential [disease-ridden]. The closeness of the place, and the heat of the climate, added to the number of the ship, which was so crowded that each had scarcely room to turn himself, almost suffocated us. This produced copious [excessive] perspirations, so that the air soon became unfit for respiration [breathing] from a variety of loathsome smells, and brought on a sickness among the slaves, of which many died—thus falling victims to the . . . avarice [greed], as I may call it, of their purchasers. This wretched situation was again aggravated by the galling [irritation] of the chains, now become insupportable [unbearable], and the filth of the necessary [waste disposal] tubs, into which the children often fell, and were almost suffocated. The shrieks of the women, and the groans of the dying, rendered [made] the whole a scene of horror almost inconceivable. Happily perhaps, for myself, I was soon reduced so low here that it was thought necessary to keep me almost always on deck; and from my extreme youth I was not put in fetters [chains]. In this situation I expected every hour to share the fate of my companions, some of whom were almost daily brought upon deck at the point of death, which I began to hope would soon put an end to my miseries. Often did I think many of the inhabitants of the deep much more happy than myself. I envied them the freedom they enjoyed, and as often wished I could change my condition for theirs. Every circumstance I met with, served only to render my state more painful, and heightened my apprehensions [fears], and my opinion of the cruelty of the whites.

   One day they had taken a number of fishes; and when they had killed and satisfied themselves with as many as they thought fit, to our astonishment

HRW material copyrighted under notice appearing earlier in this work.

who were on deck, rather than give any of them to us to eat, . . . they tossed the remaining fish into the sea again, although we begged and prayed for some as well as we could, but in vain; and some of my countrymen, being pressed by hunger, took an opportunity, when they thought no one saw them, of trying to get a little privately; but they were discovered, and the attempt procured [got] them some very severe floggings [beatings]. One day . . . two of my wearied countrymen who were chained together, (I was near them at the time,) preferring death to such a life of misery, somehow made through the nettings and jumped into the sea: immediately, another quite dejected [depressed] fellow, who, on account of his illness, was suffered [allowed] to be out of irons, also followed their example; and I believe many more would very soon have done the same, if they had not been prevented by the ship's crew, who were instantly alarmed. Those of us that were the most active, were in a moment put down under the deck, and there was such a noise and confusion amongst the people of the ship as I never heard before, to stop her, and get the boat to go out after the slaves. However, two of the wretches were drowned, but they got the other, and afterwards flogged him unmercifully, for thus attempting to prefer death to slavery. In this manner we continued to undergo more hardships than I can now relate, hardships which are inseparable from this accursed [hateful] trade. Many a time we were near suffocation from the want of fresh air, which we were often without for whole days together. This, and the stench of the necessary tubs, carried off many.

------------------------------------------------------------

From *The Interesting Narrative of the Life of Olaudah Equiano, or Gustavas Vassa, the African, Written by Himself* by Olaudah Equiano. Excerpted from *The Norton Anthology of American Literature*, third edition, Vol. I, 1989.

**UNDERSTANDING WHAT YOU READ**   After you have finished reading the selection, answer the following questions in the space provided.

**1.** What were conditions like for the enslaved Africans below deck?

_____

_____

**2.** When were the enslaved Africans allowed above deck?

_____

_____

**3.** How did the enslaved Africans try to fight against the conditions of their confinement?

_____

_____

HRW material copyrighted under notice appearing earlier in this work.

**4.** Why do you think the enslaved Africans were treated as Equiano described?

_____

_____

## ACTIVITY

Imagine that you are a newspaper editor who is opposed to the slave trade. You have just read Olaudah Equiano's account of his passages from Africa to Barbados. On a separate sheet of paper, write a newspaper editorial to persuade your readers to oppose the slave trade. You may use examples from Equiano's account to illustrate your editorial.

HRW material copyrighted under notice appearing earlier in this work.

## BIOGRAPHY READING

# Benjamin Banneker

*Not all of the African Americans who lived in the American colonies were slaves or servants. Many free African Americans ran successful businesses and made other important contributions to colonial society. Benjamin Banneker was one of these notable Americans. As a free man, Banneker was able to pursue his education and devote his time to his love of science and engineering.*

Benjamin Banneker was born in Ellicott, Maryland, in 1731. Banneker's mother had been born free, and his father had purchased his freedom some years before. Although most of the young Banneker's time was spent working on his parents' farm, during the winters he attended a nearby Quaker school. Banneker also taught himself literature, history, science, and mathematics at home.

Banneker became interested in technology after a traveling salesman gave him a pocket watch. He took the watch apart and reassembled it in order to figure out how it worked. In 1752 Banneker built a wooden clock using the pocket watch as a model. The wooden clock kept accurate time for almost 40 years. Banneker's achievement brought him a measure of local fame.

Banneker had to put his scientific and technological experiments aside when he was in his late twenties. By then he was responsible for running the family farm and had to devote all of his time to providing for his family. Later, during the American Revolution, he helped farmers build mills for grinding wheat, an important food source for American soldiers.

In the late 1780s Banneker sold the farm and devoted himself to scientific study. He spent night after night mapping the movements of the stars and planets. He also began preparing an almanac. Based on his calculations, Banneker correctly predicted that a solar eclipse would occur on April 14, 1789. Not even noted mathematicians and astronomers of the day had predicted the eclipse.

In 1789 Secretary of State Thomas Jefferson began putting together a team of surveyors and architects to plan the District of Columbia, the site of the new U.S. capital. As a surveyor, Banneker was the first African American presidential appointee. In 1792 Pierre L'Enfant, the chief city planner, left the project and took the plans with him. Banneker was able to reproduce L'Enfant's plans from memory in only two days.

In 1792 Banneker finally published his almanac. This document became the first scientific book published in the United States by an African American. The almanac included not only information about sunrises and sunsets, tides in the Chesapeake Bay, and phases of the moon, but also

HRW material copyrighted under notice appearing earlier in this work.

recipes, medical remedies, and abolitionist essays. Together with a copy of the almanac, Banneker sent a letter to Thomas Jefferson, in defense of the intellectual equality of African Americans.

About 10 years later, illness forced Banneker to stop his almanac work. Banneker died in 1806 at the age of 75. He lived his last years on a farm in Baltimore County, Maryland, where he entertained the distinguished scientists and artists of his day.

**UNDERSTANDING WHAT YOU READ** After you have finished reading the selection, answer the following questions in the space provided.

**1.** How was Benjamin Banneker educated?

_____

_____

**2.** When did Banneker become interested in science and technology?

_____

_____

**3.** What were Banneker's contributions to the development of the District of Columbia?

_____

_____

**4.** What kinds of information were included in Banneker's almanac?

_____

_____

**5.** What do you think was Banneker's greatest achievement? Why?

_____

_____

## ACTIVITY

Imagine that you are hiring someone like Benjamin Banneker to write an almanac. Create a table of contents for the almanac you will publish. You may wish to search the Internet through the HRW Go site for examples of almanacs.

 go.hrw.com

**SA1 Almanac**

HRW material copyrighted under notice appearing earlier in this work.

## Conflicts in the Colonies

★ ★ ★ ★ ★ ★ ★ ★ ★ ★ ★ ★ ★ ★ ★ ★ ★ ★ ★ ★ ★ ★ ★ ★ ★

# PRIMARY SOURCE READING

## The Outbreak of War

*In 1754 George Washington, a lieutenant colonel in the Virginia militia, led 150 soldiers into the Appalachian Mountains to investigate French activity in the region. The passage that follows is from Washington's letter to Robert Dinwiddie, governor of Virginia. The letter describes conflict between the Virginia militia and a group of French soldiers who claimed to be escorting a French ambassador to Williamsburg, the capital of Virginia. As you read the excerpt, consider the conditions under which Washington and his soldiers were fighting.*

From our Camp at the Great Meadows [Pa.]
29th of May 1754

Honble [Honorable] Sir . . .

Now Sir, as I have answer'd your Honour's Letter I shall beg leave to acqt [acquaint] you with what has happen'd since I wrote by Mr Gist; I then acquainted [informed] you that I had detach'd [sent] a party of 75 Men to meet with 50 of the French who we had Intelligence [information] were upon their March towards us . . . Abt [About] 9 Oclock the same Night, I receivd an express from the Half King[1] who was incampd with several of His People abt 6 Miles of[f], that he had seen the Tract [tracks] of two French men xing [crossing] the Road and believ'd the whole body were lying not far off . . . —I set out with 40 Men before 10, and was from that time till near Sun rise before we reach'd the Indian's Camp, havg [having] Marched in small path, & heavy Rain, and a Night as Dark as it is possible to conceive—we were frequently tumbling over one another, and often so lost that 15 or 20 Minutes search would not find the path again.

When we came to the Half King I council'd [met] with him, and got his assent to go hand in hand and strike the French; accordingly, himself, Monacatoocha, and a few other Indians set out with us, and when we came to the place where the Tracts were, the Half King sent Two Indians to follow their Tract and discover their lodgment [hiding place] which they did abt half a mile from the Road in a very obscure place surrounded with Rocks. I thereupon in conjunction [agreement] with the Half King and Monacatoocha, formd a disposion [plan] to attack them on all sides, which we accordingly did and after an Engagement of abt 15 Minutes we killd 10, wounded one and took 21 Prisoner's, amongst those that were killd was Monsieur De Jumonville the Commander, Principl Officers taken is Monsieur Druillong and Monsr Laforc, who your Honour has often heard me speak of as a bold Enterprising [ambitious] Man, and a person of gt [great] subtilty [subtlety] and cunning with these are two cadets—These Officers pretend they were coming on an Embassy, but the absurdity of the pretext is too glaring as your

HRW material copyrighted under notice appearing earlier in this work.

Honour will see by the Instructions and summons inclos'd: There Instructions were to reconnoitre [investigate] the Country, Roads, Creeks &ca [etc.] to Potomack; which they were abt to do, These Enterpriseing Men were purposely choose out [chosen] to get intelligence, which they were to send Back by some brisk dispatches with mention of the Day that they were to serve the Summon's; which could be through no other view[2], than to get sufficient Reinforcements to fall upon us immediately after. This with several other Reasons induc'd [caused] all the Officers to believe firmly that they were sent as spys rather than anything else, and has occasiond my sending them as prisoners, tho they expected (or at least had some faint hope of being continued as ambassadors). . . .

The Sense of the Half King on this Subject is, that they have bad Hearts, and that this is a mere pretence [falsehood], they never designd [planned] to have come to us but in a hostile manner, and if we were so foolish as to let them go again, he never would assist us in taking another of them. . . .

In this Engagement we had only one Man killd, and two or three wounded, among which was Lieutt [Lieutenant] Waggener slightly—a most miraculous escape, as Our Right Wing was much exposd to their Fire and receivd it all. . . .

Monsiur La-Forc, and Monsieur Druillong beg to be recommend to your Honour's Notice, and I have promis'd they will meet with all the favour that's due to Imprison'd Officers: I have shew'd [shown] all the respect I cou'd to them here, and have given some necessary cloathing by which I have disfurnish'd myself, for having brought no more than two or three Shirts from Wills Ck [Creek] . . . I was ill provided to furnish them I am Yr Honour's most Obt Hble Servt [obedient humble servant].

Go: Washington

---

From *The Papers of George Washington: Colonial Series*, Vol. 1, edited by W. W. Abbot.

**UNDERSTANDING WHAT YOU READ**   After you have finished reading the selection, answer the following questions in the space provided.

**1.** Who was allied with the Virginia militia against the French? How did this alliance strengthen Washington's position in this conflict?

_____

_____

**2.** What reasons did the captured French officers give for going to Williamsburg?

_____

_____

---

[1] American Indian leader
[2] for no other purpose

HRW material copyrighted under notice appearing earlier in this work.

**3.** What evidence made Washington disbelieve the French officers' claim?

_____

_____

**4.** How did Washington treat the captured French officers?

_____

_____

**5.** The encounter described in this letter sparked the outbreak of the French and Indian War. Based on the information provided by Washington, why might the French have considered this encounter an act of war?

_____

_____

## ACTIVITY

Imagine that you are a member of the Virginia militia, and that you have been helping to build a fort in preparation for battle against the French. Write a journal entry describing the completed fort as well as your feelings about how it will help your military efforts. You may wish to search the Internet through the HRW Go site for more information.

 go.hrw.com

**SA0 Fort Necessity**

HRW material copyrighted under notice appearing earlier in this work

**CHAPTER**

**6**

## Conflicts in the Colonies

★ ★ ★ ★ ★ ★ ★ ★ ★ ★ ★ ★ ★ ★ ★ ★ ★ ★ ★ ★ ★

# LITERATURE READING

## *Patrick Henry: The Voice of Freedom*

*In February 1775 a provincial congress was held in Massachusetts to begin preparations for a state of war. In response, the British Parliament declared Massachusetts to be in a state of rebellion. On March 23, 1775, the Virginia delegates met to discuss the issue of joining the Revolutionary War. Before the vote was taken, Patrick Henry addressed the delegates. After his power-ful speech, delegates voted for Virginia to join the American Revolution. As you read the excerpt, consider how Patrick Henry uses imagery to persuade his listeners.*

This is no time for ceremony. The question before the house is one of awful moment [great importance] to this country. For my own part I consider it as nothing less than a question of freedom or slavery; . . . Mr. President, it is nat-ural to man to indulge in the illusions of Hope.

I know of no way of judging of the future but by the past. And judging by the past, I wish to know what there has been in the conduct of the British ministry, for the last ten years, to justify those hopes with which gentlemen have been pleased to solace [comfort] themselves and the House. Is it that insidious [sly] smile with which our petition has been lately received? Trust it not, sir; it will prove a snare to your feet. Suffer not yourselves to be betrayed with a kiss. Ask yourselves how this gracious reception of our petition com-ports [goes along] with those warlike preparations which cover our waters and darken our land. . . . Let us not deceive ourselves, sir. These are the implements [tools] of war and subjugation [conquest], the last arguments to which kings resort [turn to for help]. . . . I ask gentlemen, sir, what means this martial array [display], if its purpose be not to force us into submission? . . .

They are sent over to bind and rivet [fasten firmly] upon us those chains which the British ministry have been so long forging [making]. . . . Sir, we have done everything that could be done to avert [turn away] the storm which is now coming on. . . . Our petitions have been slighted . . . and we have been spurned [pushed away] with contempt [disrespect] from the foot of the throne. . . . They tell us, sir, that we are weak ,— unable to cope with so formidable [strong] an adversary [enemy]. But when shall we be stronger? . . . Sir, we are not weak. . . . Three millions of people armed in the holy cause of liberty, and in such a country as that we possess, are invincible [cannot be conquered] by any force which our enemy can send against us. . . .

The battle, sir, is not to the strong alone: it is to the vigilant [watchful], the active, the brave. . . . There is no retreat but in submission and slavery. Our chains are forged. Their clanking may be heard on the plains of Boston. The war is inevitable. And let it come! I repeat it, sir, let it come! . . . Gentlemen may cry peace, but there is no peace. The war is actually begun.

HRW material copyrighted under notice appearing earlier in this work.

The next gale [storm] that sweeps from the north will bring to our ears the clash of . . . arms. Our brethren [brothers] are already in the field. Why stand we here idle? What is it that gentlemen wish? What would they have? Is life so dear, or peace so sweet, as to be purchased at the price of chains and slavery? Forbid it, Almighty God! I know not what course others may take, but as for me, give me liberty, or give me death!

--------------------------------------------------------------------------

From *Patrick Henry: The Voice of Freedom* by Jacob Axelrad. Copyright 1947 by Jacob Axelrad. Reprinted by permission of **Random House, Inc.**

**UNDERSTANDING WHAT YOU READ**   After you have finished reading the selection, answer the following questions in the space provided.

**1.** According to Patrick Henry, what is the important question before the Virginia House?

_____

_____

**2.** How does Henry support his claim that America is not weak? What does he believe that America has in its favor?

_____

_____

**3.** What image of slavery does Henry use in his speech?

_____

_____

**4.** According to Henry, what action would leave the colonists in a state of slavery? What action would prevent that state?

_____

_____

**ACTIVITY**

Imagine that you are creating a poster or a flyer to persuade people to support the Revolutionary War effort. On a separate sheet of paper, sketch out what the poster or flyer would look like and include either a brief account of Patrick Henry's speech or particular quotations from the speech that you find persuasive.

HRW material copyrighted under notice appearing earlier in this work.

## BIOGRAPHY READING

# Mercy Otis Warren

*Mercy Otis Warren was a historian, poet, and dramatist whose works were greatly influenced by her support of the American Revolution. She was a friend to such well-known Americans as John and Abigail Adams, Samuel Adams, and Thomas Jefferson. During the course of the Revolution, she corresponded regularly with these and other friends about the important social and political matters of the day. Warren's* A History of the Rise, Progress, and Termination of the American Revolution *offers a unique view of the American patriot cause.*

Mercy Otis was born into a wealthy Boston area family in 1728, the third of 13 children of James and Mary Otis. During her lifetime, Mercy Otis's political spirit found support in her closest relationships. Her brother James served as a king's representative until he resigned his post to oppose the writs of assistance. James Otis was also famous for his opposition to the Stamp Act. James Warren, whom Mercy Otis married in 1754 and with whom she had five sons, was a member of the Massachusetts legislature. When tensions increased in Massachusetts before the Revolutionary War, the Warren home became a meeting place for revolutionary leaders.

Warren's writings on the American Revolution provide a unique view of the times. Her sharp assessment of political events was accompanied by lively descriptions of the leading personalities of the era. Her *History* provides an analysis of the character and motives of those who opposed American independence, and is valued today for her firsthand accounts and opinions of events and people she knew personally.

After the Revolutionary War the Warren family suffered criticism for their political opinions. Mercy and James Warren, however, believed very strongly in democracy. They opposed the ratification of the U.S. Constitution because they felt it gave too much power to the federal government.

Mercy Warren endorsed the right of women to pursue interests outside of everyday domestic duties. She believed that women were not intellectually inferior to men because of their gender, but rather were intellectually inferior because they had not received the same education as men.

Mercy Warren's later years were highlighted by an argument she had with her friend John Adams. After her history of the American Revolution was published in 1805, Adams stated in a letter to Warren that he objected to her portrayal of him in the book. The two argued through a series of letters for about three months, until Warren declared that Adams's opinions were irrational. There was no contact between them for five years. Mercy Otis Warren continued to live a very active life until her death in 1814 at the age of 86.

HRW material copyrighted under notice appearing earlier in this work.

**UNDERSTANDING WHAT YOU READ**   After you have finished reading the selection, answer the following questions in the space provided.

**1.** What kinds of literary works did Warren write?

_____

_____

**2.** How did Warren become involved in the American Revolutionary cause?

_____

_____

**3.** Why did the Warrens oppose ratification of the U.S. Constitution?

_____

_____

**4.** What were some unique aspects of Warren's history of the American Revolution?

_____

_____

**5.** What was Warren's view on the role of women?

_____

_____

## ACTIVITY

Design a bulletin board that characterizes or illustrates the life of Mercy Otis Warren. Create a sketch of your bulletin board, illustrating visually the major events in Warren's life as well as her opinions about politics and women's roles. Write captions for the items on your bulletin board to explain their significance.

HRW material copyrighted under notice appearing earlier in this work.

**CHAPTER 7**

## The American Revolution

★ ★ ★ ★ ★ ★ ★ ★ ★ ★ ★ ★ ★ ★ ★ ★ ★ ★ ★ ★ ★ ★ ★ ★ ★

# PRIMARY SOURCE READING

## "On the Care of the Wounded"

*In April 1777 Dr. Benjamin Rush was appointed surgeon general of the Continental Army. He found the medical services in a terrible condition and protested to General Washington in a letter dated December 26, 1777. Rush later charged Dr. William Shippen, the director general of the medical service, with poorly managing the department. A congressional investigation cleared Shippen of the charges, after which Dr. Rush resigned from his post. The following is an excerpt of Dr. Rush's letter to General Washington. As you read the excerpt, consider the conditions under which doctors worked during the war.*

I have delayed troubling Your Excellency with the state of our hospitals in hopes you would hear it from the director general, whose business it is to correspond with Your Excellency upon this subject. . . . I beg leave therefore at last to look up to you, and through you to the Congress, as the only powers that can redress our grievances or do us justice.

I need not inform Your Excellency that we have now upward of 5,000 sick in our hospitals. This number would cease to be alarming if our hospitals could afford such accommodations to the poor fellows as would ensure them a speedy recovery. But this is far from being the case. . . . Old disorders [sicknesses] are prolonged, and new ones contracted among us. This last is so much the case that I am safe when I assert that a great majority of those who die under our hands perish [die] with diseases caught in our hospitals. . . . Every day deprives us of 4 or 5 patients out of 500 in the hospital under my care in this place. The same complaints are heard from every quarter. The surgeons have been blamed for these things, but without reason. I shall briefly point out to Your Excellency the real causes of them.

1. Too many sick are crowded together in one house. I have seen twenty sick men in one room, ill with fevers. . . .

2. The hospitals are provided in the most scanty manner with the stores [goods] necessary for sick people. . . . Beef and bread are by no means suitable diet for men in fevers.

3. There is a want [lack] of hospital shirts, sheets, and blankets to be worn by the sick. Nothing but a miracle can save the life of a soldier who lies in a shirt and blanket which he has worn for four or five months before he came into the hospital.

4. There is a want of guards and an officer to command at every hospital. . . . The men, by going out when they please, catch colds, they sell their arms, blankets, and clothes to buy rum or provisions [supplies] that are unsuitable for them . . . while within doors they quarrel and fight with each other, disobey their surgeons . . . and nurses. . . .

HRW material copyrighted under notice appearing earlier in this work.

5. The medical establishment is a bad one. . . .

The air and diet of a farmer's kitchen are the best physic [drug] in the world for a soldier worn down with the fatigues of a campaign. I have prescribed them with great success in this neighborhood, but my influence is not great enough to make the practice universal through the department. . . . Perhaps the authority of Congress may be necessary . . . to facilitate [speed up] the execution of the measure. If Your Excellency will only recommend it, I am sure it will immediately take place.

-------------------------------------------------------------------

From *Letters of Benjamin Rush*, edited by L. H. Butterfield and reprinted in *The Annals of America: Volume 2, 1755–1783*. Copyright © 1976 by Encyclopaedia Brittanica, Inc.

**UNDERSTANDING WHAT YOU READ**   After you have finished reading the selection, answer the following questions in the space provided.

**1.** How many sick lie in the hospitals? Why is this number so alarming to Dr. Rush?

_____

_____

**2.** What do a great majority of the soldiers in the hospital die of?

_____

_____

**3.** Why are more guards and officers necessary at the hospitals?

_____

_____

**4.** According to Dr. Rush, what is the best drug for worn-down soldiers?

_____

_____

**ACTIVITY**

Imagine that you are a soldier during the Revolutionary War and have been sent to one of these hospitals to recover from a battlefield wound. Write a letter home to your family about your stay in the hospital.

HRW material copyrighted under notice appearing earlier in this work.

# LITERATURE READING

## *The Crisis*

*Although the colonists had declared their independence from Great Britain on July 4, 1776, the year had been a bad one for the Continental Army. General Washington was forced to retreat through New Jersey after the crushing defeat at New York. By the fall of 1776 Washington's forces were low on supplies, and few new recruits volunteered to fight. Thomas Paine, the author of* Common Sense, *had also traveled with the retreating Continental Army. Paine hoped to use his talent as a writer to once again encourage the Patriots to continue their struggle for independence. In December Paine published the first installment of* The Crisis *in a Pennsylvania newspaper. This text was later published as a pamphlet. The document's stirring words gave the Patriots new hope. As you read the excerpt, consider how Paine tries to persuade his readers.*

These are the times that try men's souls. The summer soldier and the sunshine patriot will, in this crisis, shrink from the service of his country, but he that stands it now deserves the love and thanks of man and woman. Tyranny, like hell, is not easily conquered; yet we have this consolation [comfort] with us—that the harder the conflict, the more glorious the triumph. What we obtain too cheap, we esteem [honor] too lightly: It is dearness only that gives everything its value. Heaven knows how to put a proper price upon its goods; and it would be strange indeed if so celestial [heavenly] an article as freedom should not be highly rated. Britain, with an army to enforce her tyranny, has declared that she has a right not only to tax but "to bind us in all cases whatsoever," and if being bound in that manner is not slavery, then there is not such a thing as slavery upon earth. . . .

I turn . . . to those who have nobly stood and are yet determined to stand the matter out. I call not upon a few, but upon all; not in this state or that state, but on every state. Up and help us; . . . throw not the burden of the day upon Providence, but "show your faith by your works," that God may bless you. It matters not where you live, or what rank of life you hold, the evil or the blessing will reach you all. . . . The heart that feels not now is dead; the blood of his children will curse his cowardice who shrinks back at a time when a little might have saved the whole . . . but he whose heart is firm, and whose conscience approves his conduct, will pursue his principles unto death. . . .

There are cases which cannot be overdone by language, and this is one. There are persons, too, who see not the full extent of the evil which threatens them; they solace [assure] themselves with hopes that the enemy, if he succeed, will be merciful. It is the madness of folly to expect mercy from those who have refused to do justice. . . .

HRW material copyrighted under notice appearing earlier in this work.

By perseverance [determination] and fortitude [endurance] we have the prospect of a glorious issue [result]; by cowardice and submission, the sad choice of a variety of evils—a ravaged country—a depopulated city—habitations [homes] without safety and slavery without hope. . . . Look on this picture and weep over it! And if there yet remains one thoughtless wretch who believes it not, let him suffer it unlamented [without grief].

---

From *The Political Writings of Thomas Paine*, reprinted in *The Annals of America: Volume 2, 1755–1783*. Copyright © 1976 by Encyclopaedia Brittanica, Inc.

**UNDERSTANDING WHAT YOU READ**   After you have finished reading the selection, answer the following questions in the space provided.

**1.** What is the main idea of *The Crisis*?

_____

_____

**2.** How does Paine try to persuade his readers?

_____

_____

**3.** What does Paine mean by "the summer soldier and the sunshine patriot"?

_____

_____

**4.** At the end of the first paragraph, why does Paine quote the words of the British directly?

_____

_____

**5.** What does Paine say will happen if people do not support the fight against the British?

_____

_____

**ACTIVITY**

On a separate sheet of paper, create a book jacket that might have accompanied *The Crisis* when it was first published. Your book jacket should capture the main idea of the book and the reason it was written.

HRW material copyrighted under notice appearing earlier in this work.

# BIOGRAPHY READING

# Paul Revere

*Paul Revere was a relatively unknown figure in American history until 1863, when Henry Wadsworth Longfellow published a somewhat historically inaccurate poem about his midnight ride. Soon after, silver items made by Paul Revere increased dramatically in value and the owner of Revere's famous Sons of Liberty punch bowl was offered $100,000 for its sale. Yet, there is much more to Paul Revere's life than his dramatic midnight ride on April 19, 1775.*

Paul Revere was born in Boston, Massachusetts, in 1735. He studied to be a silversmith but later learned other trades when the silversmithing trade became overcrowded in Boston. Revere's later trades included engraving portraits, making bookplates, writing political cartoons, and manufacturing dental devices. In fact, some people believe that Revere may have made a set of false teeth for George Washington.

In 1773 Revere helped organize the Boston Tea Party and was one of the men who dressed up as Mohawk Indians to throw British tea overboard from East India Company ships. He then rode from Boston to New York City in the middle of the winter to inform the Sons of Liberty of the event.

In the spring of 1774 Revere rode to New York City and Philadelphia with news of the Boston Port Bill, which prohibited the loading and unloading of ships in any part of Boston Harbor. Later, Revere was appointed official courier to the Continental Congress for the Massachusetts Provincial Congress.

Two days before Revere made his famous ride to Lexington and Concord to announce the British invasion, he rode to Concord to warn patriots to move their military supplies from the town. When the Boston Committee of Safety learned of the planned British advance on the area, its members sent Revere and William Dawes to alert the countryside. Revere reached Lexington at midnight on April 19, 1775, and warned Samuel Adams and John Hancock so they could avoid capture by the British. After warning the other colonists, Revere was captured by a British patrol, questioned, and later released.

Once the war began, Revere's work included such varied tasks as designing and printing the first issue of Continental currency, learning and supervising the process of manufacturing gunpowder, and making the first official seal for the colonies, as well as one for Massachusetts that is still in use today.

Revere became a major of militia on April 10, 1776, and was promoted to lieutenant colonel that same year. His opportunity for field duty came when he took command at Castle William from 1778 to 1779. Toward the end of 1778, Revere was put in charge of three remaining artillery companies that

HRW material copyrighted under notice appearing earlier in this work.

remained in Boston. On September 6, 1779, Revere was relieved of his duty at Castle William and charged with disobedience, unsoldierly conduct, and cowardice. He was later found not guilty.

Revere later returned to his trades and also worked for the ratification of the U.S. Constitution. He invented the process for rolling sheet copper and opened a mill at Canton, Massachusetts. Paul Revere died in 1818 at the age of 83.

**UNDERSTANDING WHAT YOU READ** After you have finished reading the selection, answer the following questions in the space provided.

**1.** List three of Paul Revere's trades.

_____

_____

**2.** What role did Revere play in the Boston Tea Party?

_____

_____

**3.** Why did Revere ride to Concord on April 17, 1775?

_____

_____

**4.** What were Revere's nonmilitary contributions to the war effort?

_____

_____

**5.** What was Revere charged with after he was relieved of his duty at Castle William?

_____

_____

**ACTIVITY**

On a separate sheet of paper, sketch or draw a scene of one of the events of Paul Revere's life. Then write a two- or three-sentence caption that explains the scene you have drawn.

HRW material copyrighted under notice appearing earlier in this work.

# PRIMARY SOURCE READING

## Iroquois *Great Law of Peace*

*The Iroquois* Great Law of Peace *was a constitution that established a democracy among five Iroquois-speaking tribes—the Seneca, Cayuga, Oneida, Onondaga, and Mohawk. This group of five nations, called the Iroquois Confederacy, was established around 1450. The* Great Law of Peace *was thought to have been produced shortly after the Iroquois Confederacy was formed, and was recorded on wampum belts, or belts made with ornamental shells. The original purpose of this constitution was to end years of bloody battle among these five nations. As you read the following excerpt, think about how the confederacy made decisions.*

2. Roots have spread out from the Tree of the Great Peace, one to the north, one to the east, one to the south and one to the west. The name of these roots is the Great White Roots and their nature is Peace and Strength.

   If any man or any nation outside the Five Nations shall obey the laws of the Great Peace and shall make their disposition [swear their allegiance] to the Lords of the Confederacy, they may trace the Roots to the Tree and if their minds are clean and they are obedient and promise to obey the wishes of the Confederate Council, they shall be welcomed to take shelter beneath the Tree of the Long Leaves.

5. The council of the Mohawk shall be divided into three parties as follows: Tekarihoken, Ayonhwhathah, and Skadekariwade are the first party; Sharenhowaneh, Deyoenhegwehn and Oghrenghrehgowah the second party, and Kehennakrineh, Aghstawenserrenthah and Shoskoharowaneh are the third party. The third party is to listen only to the discussion of the first and second parties and if an error is made or the proceeding is irregular they are to call attention to it, and when the case is right and properly decided by the two parties they shall confirm the decision of the two parties and refer the case to the Seneca Lords for their decision. When the Seneca Lords have decided in accord [agreement] with the Mohawk Lords, the case or question shall be referred to the Cayuga and Oneida Lords on the opposite side of the house.

16. If the conditions which arise at any future time call for an addition to or change of this law, the case shall be carefully considered and if a new beam [law] seems necessary or beneficial, the proposed change shall be voted upon and if adopted shall be called, "Added to the Rafter."

24. The chiefs of the League of Five Nations shall be mentors of the people for all time. The thickness of their skins shall be seven spans, which is to say that they shall be proof against anger, offensive action and criticism. Their hearts shall be full of peace and good will and their minds filled with a yearning for the welfare of the people of the league. With endless patience, they shall carry out their duty. Their firmness shall be tempered with a tenderness for their people.

HRW material copyrighted under notice appearing earlier in this work.

92. If a nation, part of a nation, or more than one nation within the Five Nations should in any way endeavor [try] to destroy the Great Peace by neglect or violating its laws and resolve to dissolve the Confederacy such a nation or such nations shall be deemed guilty of treason and called enemies of the Confederacy and the Great Peace.

93. Whenever a specially important matter or a great emergency is presented before the Confederate Council and the nature of the matter affects the entire body of Five Nations threatening their utter [complete] ruin, then the Lords of the Confederacy must submit the matter to the decision of their people and the decision of the people shall affect the decision of the Confederate Council. This decision shall be a confirmation of the voice of the people.

94. The men of every clan of the Five Nations shall have a Council Fire ever burning in readiness for a council of the clan. When it seems necessary for a council to be held to discuss the welfare of the clans, then the men may gather about the fire. This council shall have the same rights as the council of the women.

95. The women of every clan of the Five Nations shall have a Council Fire ever burning in readiness for a council of the clan. When in their opinion it seems necessary for the interest of the people they shall hold a council and their decision and recommendation shall be introduced before the Council of Lords by the War Chief for its consideration.

------------------------------------------------------------

From *The Iroquois and the Founding of the American Nation* by Donald A. Grinde, Jr. Copyright © 1977 by *The Indian Historian Press, Inc.* Reprinted by permission of the publisher.

**UNDERSTANDING WHAT YOU READ**    After you have finished reading the selection, answer the following questions in the space provided.

**1.** According to the excerpt, who approves decisions made by the Mohawk council?

_____

_____

**2.** How is a new law added to the Great Law of Peace? What is the term for the new law?

_____

_____

**3.** What are some of the requirements of a chief in the League of Five Nations?

_____

_____

**ACTIVITY**

Imagine that you are listening to the discussion of the five tribes before the adoption of the Great Law of Peace. On a separate sheet of paper, list what you think may have been arguments for and arguments against the creation of the Iroquois Confederacy.

HRW material copyrighted under notice appearing earlier in this work.

## LITERATURE READING

# A View of America

*J. Hector St. John de Crèvecoeur was an American farmer who wrote a series of letters to a friend in Europe describing some unique characteristics of America. He wrote these letters to provide information to people on "the other side of the Atlantic" about the unusual nature and special qualities of American society. The book's introduction noted that the farmer "has severely felt, the desolating consequences of a rupture between the parent state [England] and her colonies," which indicates that he probably sided with the English during the Revolutionary War. As you read the excerpt, think about how Crèvecoeur describes the differences between Americans and Europeans.*

LETTER III.

WHAT IS AN AMERICAN.

I WISH I could be acquainted with the feelings and thoughts which must agitate [disturb] the heart and present themselves to the mind of an enlightened [knowledgeable] Englishman, when he first lands on this continent. He must greatly rejoice that he lived at a time to see this fair country discovered and settled; he must necessarily feel a share of national pride, when he views the chain of settlements which embellishes [decorates] these extended shores. When he says to himself, this is the work of my countrymen, who . . . took refuge [shelter] here. They brought along with them their national genius, to which they principally owe what liberty they enjoy, and what substance they possess. Here he sees the industry of his native country displayed in a new manner, and traces in their works the embrios [beginnings] of all the arts, sciences, and ingenuity [cleverness] which flourish in Europe.

He is arrived on a new continent; a modern society offers itself to his contemplation [thought], different from what he had . . . seen. It is not composed [made], as in Europe, of great lords who possess every thing and of a herd of people who have nothing. Here are no aristocratical [upper class] families, no courts, no kings, no bishops, no ecclesiastical [religious] dominion, no invisible power giving to a few a very visible one; no great manufacturers employing thousands, no great . . . luxury. The rich and the poor are not so far removed from each other as they are in Europe . . . We are a people of cultivators [farmers], scattered over an immense territory communicating with each other by means of good roads and navigable rivers, united by the silken bands of mild government, all respecting the laws, without dreading their power, because they are equitable [equal]. We are all animated with the spirit of an industry which is . . . unrestrained, because each person works for himself.

The next wish of this traveller will be to know whence [from where] came all these people? They are a mixture of English, Scotch, Irish, French, Dutch,

HRW material copyrighted under notice appearing earlier in this work.

Germans, and Swedes. From this . . . that race now called Americans have arisen. The eastern provinces must indeed be excepted, as being the unmixed descendants of Englishmen. . . . In this great American asylum, the poor of Europe have by some means met together, and in consequence of various causes; to what purpose should they ask one another what countrymen they are? Alas, two thirds of them had no country. Can a wretch [miserable person] who wanders about, who works and starves, whose life is a continual scene of sore affliction [misfortune] or pinching penury [poverty]; can that man call England or any other kingdom his country? . . . Formerly they were not numbered in any civil lists of their country, except in those of the poor; here they rank as citizens. By what invisible power has this surprising metamorphosis [change] been performed? By that of the laws and that of their industry. The laws, the indulgent laws, protect them as they arrive, stamping on them the symbol of adoption; they receive ample rewards for their labours; these accumulated rewards procure them lands; those lands confer on [give] them the title of freemen, and to that title every benefit is affixed [attached] which men can possibly require. This is the great operation daily performed by our laws . . . . What then is the American, this new man? . . . *He* is an American, who leaving behind him all his ancient prejudices and manners, receives new ones from the new mode of life he has embraced, the new government he obeys, and the new rank he holds.

---

From *Letters From An American Farmer,* by J. Hector St. John de Crèvecoeur, reprinted from the original ed., with a prefatory note by W. P. Trent and an introduction by Ludwig Lewisohn. Copyright 1904.

**UNDERSTANDING WHAT YOU READ**   After you have finished reading the selection, answer the following questions in the space provided.

**1.** According to Crèvecoeur, why should an Englishman be proud of America?

_____

_____

**2.** How does Crèvecoeur feel that American society is different from European society?

_____

_____

**3.** How does Crèvecoeur characterize the people who have settled in America? What were their reasons for leaving Europe?

_____

_____

HRW material copyrighted under notice appearing earlier in this work.

**4.** What does Crèvecoeur list as the metamorphosis, or change, that is central to obtaining freedom in America? How is this process ensured?

_____

_____

## ACTIVITY

Imagine that you are writing a biographical dictionary. Create a half-page entry about J. Hector St. John de Crèvecoeur. You may wish to search the Internet through the HRW Go site for more information.

 **go.hrw.com**

**SA1 De Crèvecoeur**

HRW material copyrighted under notice appearing earlier in this work.

**Forming a Government**

★ ★ ★ ★ ★ ★ ★ ★ ★ ★ ★ ★ ★ ★ ★ ★ ★ ★ ★ ★ ★ ★ ★ ★ ★ ★ ★

## BIOGRAPHY READING

# George Mason

*George Mason was a planter from Virginia who became a great statesman and was a strong supporter of the U.S. Constitution. Although Mason was often reluctant to take an active public role in the American Revolution, he helped inspire the revolutionary cause and played an important role at the Constitutional Convention.*

George Mason was born in 1725 into a wealthy family in Fairfax County, Virginia. Because his father had died, Mason grew up under the care of his mother, Ann, and his uncle, John Mercer, a well-respected lawyer. Mason learned much from his uncle's library, which contained many books on law. He married Anne Eilbeck in 1750, and the couple had five sons and four daughters.

Mason was very involved in local government and the church, serving as a trustee of Alexandria, a justice of the Fairfax County court, and a vestryman of Truro Parish. Mason also was a member of the Ohio Company and served as its treasurer until 1773. Mason also managed his 5,000-acre plantation alone.

During the American Revolution Mason played a supporting role. Behind the scenes he thought of ways people could avoid paying the taxes required by the Stamp Act, Townsend Acts, and other taxes that Britain had imposed on the American colonists. In 1775 he came out of political retirement to serve in the various Virginia conventions. For example, he served on the Committee of Safety, which was in charge of getting weapons for the militia. Mason helped draft Virginia's Declaration of Rights—which Thomas Jefferson used to write the first part of the Declaration of Independence—and the Virginia constitution.

Mason represented Virginia at the 1787 Constitutional Convention in Philadelphia, where he was one of the five most frequent speakers. He refused to sign the final version of the Constitution because it lacked a bill of rights. Mason served at the Virginia ratifying convention in June 1788, and he continued to call for a defeat of the Constitution as it was written. In spite of his efforts, Virginia ratified the Constitution in a close vote.

Mason later introduced the set of 10 amendments that would become the Bill of Rights, at which time he announced his readiness to "chearfully put my Hand & Heart to the new Government." He later refused a seat in the Senate, saying that he needed to attend to his health and to family matters. Mason died in 1792 at the age of 67.

HRW material copyrighted under notice appearing earlier in this work.

**UNDERSTANDING WHAT YOU READ**   After you have finished reading the selection, answer the following questions in the space provided.

**1.** In what ways was Mason involved in his local government?

_____

_____

**2.** How did Mason support the American Revolution?

_____

_____

**3.** List some of the important documents Mason helped draft.

_____

_____

**4.** Why did Mason refuse to put his signature on the newly written U.S. Constitution?

_____

_____

## ACTIVITY

Imagine that you are a newspaper reporter who is interviewing delegates to the Constitutional Convention. Find a partner in your class and plan a mock interview in which one of you plays the newspaper reporter and the other plays George Mason. Write down the questions that you will ask about Mason's life and his involvement with the creation of the U.S. Constitution, including why he refused to sign. Then write down "Mason's" responses to the questions. Present your dramatization to the class.

HRW material copyrighted under notice appearing earlier in this work.

**CHAPTER**
**9**

## Citizenship and the Constitution

★ ★ ★ ★ ★ ★ ★ ★ ★ ★ ★ ★ ★ ★ ★ ★ ★ ★ ★ ★ ★ ★ ★ ★

# PRIMARY SOURCE READING

## Antifederalists

*Although the Constitution was eventually ratified by all 13 states, citizens engaged in heated public debates about its adoption. Supporters and opponents of the Constitution carried on their debates in a series of letters and editorials that were published in many newspapers. Most of the articles were written under pseudonyms, or false names, that kept the writer's identity a secret. Supporters of the Constitution, known as Federalists, and opponents of the Constitution, known as Antifederalists, argued about the meaning of the Constitution and its power to create a strong central government. Although the Federalists eventually convinced a majority of citizens to support the Constitution, Antifederalists raised significant questions that are still discussed today. In this selection from Antifederalist No. 17, one of the most brilliant of the Antifederalist writers, BRUTUS, predicts exactly how and why federal powers would increase, through an interpretation of the necessary and proper clause in the Constitution. As you read this excerpt, consider which of BRUTUS's arguments were most convincing, and which might still raise questions today.*

This [new] government is to possess absolute [complete] and uncontrollable powers, legislative, executive, and judicial, with respect to every object to which it extends, for by the last clause of section eighth, article first, it is declared, that the Congress shall have power "to make all laws which shall be necessary and proper for carrying into execution the foregoing [previous] powers, and all other powers vested by this Constitution in the government of the United States, or in any department or office thereof." It appears from these articles, that there is no need of any intervention of the State governments, between the Congress and the people, to execute [carry out] any one power vested in [held by] the general government, and that the Constitution and laws of every State are nullified [canceled] and declared void, so far as they are or shall be inconsistent with this Constitution, or the laws made in pursuance [support] of it, or with treaties made under the authority of the United States. The government, then, so far as it extends, is a complete one, and not a confederation. It is as much one complete government as that of New York or Massachusetts; has as absolute and perfect powers to make and execute all laws, to appoint officers, institute courts, declare offenses, and annex [take control of] penalties, with respect to every object to which it extends, as any other in the world. So far, therefore, as its powers reach, all ideas of confederation are given up and lost. It is true this government is limited to certain objects, or to speak more properly, some small degree of power is still left to the States; but a little attention to the powers vested in the general government, will convince every candid [honest] man, that if it is capable of being executed, all that is reserved for the individual States must very soon be

HRW material copyrighted under notice appearing earlier in this work.

annihilated [destroyed], except so far as they are barely necessary to the organization of the general government. The powers of the general legislature extend to every case that is of the least importance—there is nothing valuable to human nature, nothing dear to freemen, but what is within its power. It has the authority to make laws which will affect the lives, the liberty, and property of every man in the United States; nor can the Constitution or laws of any State, in any way prevent . . . the full and complete execution of every power given. But what is meant is, that the legislature of the United States are vested with [given] the great and uncontrollable powers of laying and collecting taxes, duties, . . . regulating trade, raising and supporting armies, organizing, arming, and disciplining the militia, instituting courts, and other general powers; and are by this clause invested with the power of making all laws, proper and necessary, for carrying all these into execution; and they may exercise this power as entirely to annihilate all the State governments, and reduce this country to one single government. . . . [I]t is a truth confirmed by the unerring [accurate] experience of ages, that every man, and every body of men, invested with power, are ever disposed to increase it, and to acquire a superiority over everything that stands in their way.

---

From *The Antifederalist Papers,* ed. with an introduction by Morton Borden. Copyright © 1965 by Michigan State University Press.

**UNDERSTANDING WHAT YOU READ**   After you have finished reading the selection, answer the following questions in the space provided.

**1.** What part of the Constitution is the author concerned with in this selection?

_____

_____

**2.** Does the author think that the federal government will be a confederation of the separate states?

_____

_____

**3.** What does the author think will eventually happen to the power of individual states under the new federal system?

_____

_____

**4.** What are some of the "great and uncontrollable" powers of the new federal government listed by the author?

_____

_____

HRW material copyrighted under notice appearing earlier in this work.

**5.** What is the principle of human behavior that the author points to as a reason not to give so much power to a central government?

_____

_____

## ACTIVITY

On a separate sheet of paper, draw either a cartoon or a short comic strip that illustrates what would happen to state governments under a new federal system according to the author's prediction in the reading.

HRW material copyrighted under notice appearing earlier in this work.

**CHAPTER**
**9**

## Citizenship and the Constitution

★ ★ ★ ★ ★ ★ ★ ★ ★ ★ ★ ★ ★ ★ ★ ★ ★ ★ ★ ★ ★ ★ ★ ★

# LITERATURE READING

## *The Free Citizen*

*One of the most outspoken leaders on the topic of popular self-government was President Theodore Roosevelt, who held office from 1901 to 1909. Roosevelt was dedicated to the belief that each American needed to be educated and trained in order to be an effective citizen. Roosevelt's personal moral and political philosophy about free government affected his actions as both a leader and an average citizen. As you read the following excerpt from* The Free Citizen, *notice the ways in which Roosevelt thinks Americans should be good citizens.*

1. *We carry the responsibility for our government. . . .*

Men can never escape being governed. Either they must govern themselves or they must submit to being governed by others. If from lawlessness or fickleness [changing one's mind] . . . they refuse to govern themselves, then most assuredly in the end they will have to be governed from the outside. They can prevent the need of government from without only by showing that they possess the power of government from within. . . .

Are the American people fit to govern themselves? . . . I believe they are. . . . I believe the majority of the plain people of the United States will, day in and day out, make fewer mistakes in governing themselves than any smaller class or body of men, no matter what their training, will make in trying to govern them. In spite of all our failings and shortcomings, we of this Republic have more nearly realized than any other people on earth the ideal of justice attained through genuine popular rule.

2. *. . . not for the sake only of our own country's future. . . .*

The history of America is now the central feature of the history of the world; for the world has set its face hopefully toward our democracy; and, O my fellow citizens, each one of you carries on your shoulders not only the burden of doing well for the sake of your own country, but the burden of doing well and of seeing that this nation does well for the sake of mankind. Nowhere else in all the world is there such a chance for the triumph on a gigantic scale of the great cause of democratic and popular government. If we fail, the failure will be lamentable [sad] . . . for not only shall we fail for ourselves, but our failure will wreck the fond desires of all throughout the world who look toward us with the hope that here in this great Republic it shall be proved from ocean to ocean that the people can rule themselves, and thus ruling can gain liberty for and do justice both to themselves and to others. Our success means not only our own triumph, but the triumph of the cause of the rights of the people throughout the world, and the uplifting of the banner of hope for all the nations of mankind.

HRW material copyrighted under notice appearing earlier in this work.

3. *. . . and we must be trained to bear it if freedom is to survive.*

The democratic ideal must be that of subordinating chaos to order . . . the individual to the community . . . of training every man to realize that no one is entitled to citizenship in a great free commonwealth unless he does his full duty to his neighbor, his full duty to his family life, and his full duty to the nation.

The republic cannot succeed if we do not take pains in educating the masters of the  republic. . . . It is easy enough to live under a despotism [without freedom].  You do not have to do anything; just let the other man govern. But it is not easy to live in a republic where each man has to do his part in the governing, and where he cannot do it if there is not a sound basis of moral and intellectual training . . . steady training . . . in conscience and character, until he grows to abhor [hate] corruption and greed and tyranny and brutality and to prize justice and fair dealing. . . .

Failure to train the average citizen . . . must in the long run entail [involve] misfortune, shortcoming, possible disaster, upon the Nation itself.

------------------------------------------------------------

From *The Free Citizen,* by Theodore Roosevelt, ed. by Hermann Hagedorn. Copyright © 1956 by The Theodore Roosevelt Association.

**UNDERSTANDING WHAT YOU READ**   After you have finished reading the selection, answer the following questions in the space provided.

**1.** According to Theodore Roosevelt, what character traits do people need to possess in order to govern themselves?

_____

_____

**2.** Why did Roosevelt believe that the history of America is central to the history of the world?

_____

_____

**3.** According to Roosevelt, what will happen if Americans cannot make democracy succeed?

_____

_____

**4.** What did Roosevelt say that people must do in order to be entitled to full citizenship?

_____

_____

HRW material copyrighted under notice appearing earlier in this work.

**5.** How important do you think education was to Roosevelt? What did he think would happen if citizens were not effectively educated?

_____

_____

## ACTIVITY

Imagine that you are a book critic for a newspaper. Write a review of Roosevelt's _Free Citizen_, focusing on this excerpt. Remember to include an analysis of how Roosevelt expresses his ideas as well as your opinion of those ideas.

HRW material copyrighted under notice appearing earlier in this work.

## Citizenship and the Constitution

★ ★ ★ ★ ★ ★ ★ ★ ★ ★ ★ ★ ★ ★ ★ ★ ★ ★ ★ ★ ★ ★ ★ ★ ★

## BIOGRAPHY READING

# John Jay

*John Jay is best known as the first chief justice of the U.S. Supreme Court. That appointment, however, was only one achievement in the life of this statesman, diplomat, and highly regarded leader. Jay served the new nation in many roles.*

John Jay was born in New York City in 1745, the sixth son of Peter and Mary Jay. As a boy, Jay was tutored at home. He enjoyed his studies, and in 1764 he graduated from King's College (now Columbia University). Jay then began to prepare for the bar in the New York law office of Benjamin Kissum.

In 1768 Jay passed the bar exam and became a lawyer. He married Sarah Van Brugh Livingston on April 28, 1774. The couple had two sons and five daughters. The American Revolution brought an end to Jay's legal career, and he began a career of public service. He helped to write the constitution of the state of New York and served as the state's chief justice until 1779. He also was New York's representative to the First and Second Continental Congresses. In 1778 Jay was elected president of the Second Continental Congress, a position he held until September 1779 when he was sent on a diplomatic mission to Spain.

Jay asked the Spanish government to recognize American independence and provide financial support to the new nation. Although the Spanish would not officially recognize the United States, they did provide money and weapons in secret. In 1782 Benjamin Franklin called Jay to Paris to help with the peace negotiations with Great Britain. The terms of the peace treaty were settled in 1783.

After the war ended, Jay refused appointments as minister to Great Britain and as minister to France because he wanted to return to private life in New York. Congress, however, had already appointed him secretary of foreign affairs. Jay accepted the appointment and remained in that office until after the Constitution was adopted and the government reorganized. Although he did not attend the Constitutional Convention, he wrote five essays in support of ratification.

President George Washington nominated Jay to be the first chief justice of the Supreme Court. The most important case decided by Jay was *Chisholm* v. *Georgia*. In his decision Jay said that a citizen of one state had the right to sue another state. Because the states did not agree with his decision, they quickly passed the Eleventh Amendment to the Constitution to protect states from being sued.

HRW material copyrighted under notice appearing earlier in this work.

While serving as chief justice, Jay was sent to Great Britain to resolve a new crisis. The British navy had seized U.S. ships carrying illegal goods from the French West Indies. Jay negotiated a treaty to resolve many of the problems between the two countries. On his return to the United States he resigned his post as chief justice to serve as governor of New York. After serving two terms as governor, he retired from politics. Jay refused a nomination by President Adams to serve as chief justice a second time, and spent the rest of his life in retirement. He died in 1829 at the age of 84.

**UNDERSTANDING WHAT YOU READ**  After you have finished reading the selection, answer the following questions in the space provided.

**1.** What event brought an end to John Jay's legal career?

_____

_____

**2.** Why was Jay sent to Spain? What was the outcome of his trip?

_____

_____

**3.** What did Jay decide in *Chisholm* v. *Georgia*? Why did Congress pass the Eleventh Amendment?

_____

_____

**4.** What did Jay do after he resigned his post as chief justice?

_____

_____

**ACTIVITY**

Imagine that you are a friend who has been invited to give a eulogy at the funeral of John Jay. On a separate sheet of paper, write out the short speech you would give about Jay's life and his many contributions to the country.

HRW material copyrighted under notice appearing earlier in this work.

# *Democracy in America*

*As the United States developed, people in countries around the world became interested in this experiment in democracy. The French felt a special kinship to the United States because the American Revolution had encouraged French citizens to revolt against their own government. In 1831 Alexis de Tocqueville traveled from France to visit the United States. Soon after, he published a book,* Democracy in America, *in which he tried to illustrate how democracy and equality affected political life, family life, literature, philosophy, intellectual pursuits, trade, and everyday manners in the United States. While reading this excerpt from Tocqueville's book, notice how he describes his perception of this relationship between democracy and everyday life in the United States.*

I think that in no country in the civilized world is less attention paid to philosophy than in the United States. The Americans have no philosophical school of their own, and they care but little for all the schools into which Europe is divided, the very names of which are scarcely known to them.

Yet it is easy to perceive that almost all the inhabitants of the United States use their minds in the same manner, and direct them according to the same rules; that is to say, without ever having taken the trouble to define the rules, they have a philosophical method common to the whole people.

To evade [escape] the bondage of system and habit, of family maxims [sayings], class opinions, and, in some degree, of national prejudices [unreasonable opinions]; to accept tradition only as a means of information, and existing facts only as a lesson to be used in doing otherwise and doing better; to seek the reason of things for oneself, and in oneself alone; to tend to results without being bound to means, and to strike through the form to the substance—such are the principal characteristics of what I shall call the philosophical method of the Americans.

But if I go further and seek among these characteristics the principal one, which includes almost all the rest, I discover that in most of the operations of the mind each American appeals only to the individual effort of his own understanding. . . .

The practice of Americans leads their minds to other habits, to fixing the standard of their judgment in themselves alone. As they perceive that they succeed in resolving [solving] without assistance all the little difficulties which their practical life presents, they readily conclude that everything in the world may be explained, and that nothing in it transcends [goes beyond] the limits of the understanding. Thus they fall to denying what they cannot comprehend [understand]; which leaves them but little faith for whatever is extraordinary. . . .

HRW material copyrighted under notice appearing earlier in this work.

There are no revolutions that do not shake existing belief, enervate [weaken] authority, and throw doubts over commonly received ideas. Every revolution has more or less the effect of releasing men to their own conduct and of opening before the mind of each one of them an almost limitless perspective. When equality of conditions succeeds [follows] a protracted [lengthy] conflict between the different classes of which the elder society was composed, envy, hatred, and uncharitableness, pride and exaggerated self-confidence seize upon the human heart, and plant their sway for a time. This, independently of equality itself, tends powerfully to divide men, to lead them to mistrust the judgment of one another, and to seek the light of truth nowhere but in themselves. Everyone then attempts to be his own sufficient guide and makes it his boast to form his own opinions on all subjects. Men are no longer bound together by ideas, but by interests.

-----

From *Democracy in America* by Alexis de Tocqueville. Copyright 1945 and renewed © 1973 by **Alfred A. Knopf, Inc.** Reprinted by permission of the publisher.

**UNDERSTANDING WHAT YOU READ** After you have finished reading the selection, answer the following questions in the space provided.

**1.** According to Alexis de Tocqueville, what are some of the "rules" that influence the thinking of Americans?

_____

_____

**2.** What is "the philosophical method of the Americans," according to Tocqueville?

_____

_____

**3.** According to Tocqueville, what are some of the pitfalls of relying strictly on individual judgment?

_____

_____

**4.** How does Tocqueville identify the ultimate results of revolutions?

_____

_____

HRW material copyrighted under notice appearing earlier in this work.

**5.** What do you think Tocqueville meant when he said that "men are no longer bound together by ideas, but by interests"?

_____

_____

## ACTIVITY

Imagine that you are writing a travel brochure that describes either a country or a particular state. On a separate sheet of paper, write a paragraph that describes the unique characteristics of the citizens, such as their outlook on life, way of thinking, or other special attributes. You may wish to search the Internet through the HRW Go site for examples of state travel information.

go.hrw.com

**SA1 Travel**

HRW material copyrighted under notice appearing earlier in this work.

## LITERATURE READING

# *The Coquette*

*The early American novel was similar to novels being written in England. Both were usually tales of love and romance that were told with a highly moral tone. Most readers of these novels were young women, who chose them in spite of discouragement from educators, clergymen, and the editors of women's magazines.* The Coquette *was an early American novel in which the story was told through a series of letters written by major and minor characters. As you read the following excerpt, notice how the author of the story hoped to prevent her readers from making bad moral choices by showing them the consequences that characters suffered for immoral behavior.*

Letter XXX

To Miss Lucy Freeman.                                                                New Haven

I believe your spirits need a cordial [tonic] indeed, my dear Lucy, after drawing so dreadful a portrait of my swain [suitor]. But I call him mine no longer. I renounce him entirely. My friends shall be gratified; and if their predictions are verified [proved true], I shall be happy in a union [marriage] with a man of their choice. . . .

Thus terminated [ended] this affair [relationship]—an affair which, perhaps, was only the effect of mere gallantry [politeness] on his part, and of unmeaning pleasantry on mine. I am sorry to say that it has given my friends so much anxiety and concern. I am under obligations to them for their kind solicitude [loving care], however causeless it may have been.

Eliza Wharton.

Letter XXXI

To Miss Eliza Wharton.                                                                Hartford

I am very happy to find you are in so good spirits, Eliza, after parting with your favorite swain [suitor]; for I perceive that he is really the favorite of your fancy, though your heart cannot esteem [respect] him. . . .

I can tell you some news of this strange man. He has arrived and taken possession of his seat [house]. Having given general invitations, he has been called upon and welcomed by most of the neighboring gentry. Yesterday he made an elegant entertainment. Friend George (as you call him) and I were of the number who had cards. Twenty-one couples went, I am told. We did not go. I consider my time too valuable to be spent in cultivating [developing] acquaintance with a person from whom neither pleasure nor improvement is to be expected. . . .

HRW material copyrighted under notice appearing earlier in this work.

I look upon the vicious habits and abandoned character of Major Sanford to have more pernicious [harmful] effects on society than the perpetrations [crimes] of the robber and the assassin. These, when detected, are rigidly punished by the laws of the land. . . . But, to the disgrace of humanity and virtue [goodness], the assassin of honor, the wretch [miserable person] . . . is received . . . not only by his own sex [men] . . . but even by ours [women], who have every conceivable [imaginable] reason to despise and avoid him. . . . I am neither ashamed nor afraid openly to avow [declare] my sentiments [opinions] of this man and my reasons for treating him with the most pointed neglect.

Lucy Freeman.

From *The Coquette*, by Mrs. Hannah W. Foster, ed. by William S. Osborne. Copyright © 1970 by College and University Press Services, Inc.

**UNDERSTANDING WHAT YOU READ**   After you have finished reading the selection, answer the following questions in the space provided.

**1.** With whom does Eliza Wharton say she has broken off a relationship? What reasons does she give for her decision?

_____

_____

**2.** Why is Eliza sorry that she was in this relationship?

_____

_____

**3.** Does Lucy Freeman believe that Eliza is happy that the relationship is over?

_____

_____

**4.** What does Lucy think of Major Sanford?

_____

_____

**ACTIVITY**

Imagine that you are a close friend or relative of Lucy Freeman. Write her a letter suggesting that she advise Eliza Wharton how to act next time she encounters Major Sanford.

HRW material copyrighted under notice appearing earlier in this work.

# BIOGRAPHY READING

## Judith Sargent Murray

*Judith Sargent Murray was the author of many literary works. In her writing she argues that men and women are intellectual equals, and calls for more complete education for girls. Murray also believed that if a girl is encouraged to develop a good image of self, she will avoid rushing into marriage simply to gain status or to avoid a life without a husband.*

Judith Sargent Murray was born in 1751. She was the first of eight children born to Winthrop and Judith Sargent, who lived in Gloucester, Massachusetts. Her father was a successful merchant and shipowner. Her brother was a hero in the Revolutionary War and later became the first governor of the Mississippi Territory.

As a teenager, Judith Sargent was educated alongside her brother as he prepared to attend Harvard. On breaks from Harvard, he taught his older sister what he was learning. Judith Sargent met John Stevens, a sea captain and trader, and in October of 1769 they were married.

Judith Sargent Stevens decided she wanted to be a writer. She began writing some poetry, but as the social and political events leading up to the American Revolution unfolded, she began writing essays. Many of the questions about liberty and human rights that were being argued among patriots led her to think about the rights and roles of women. In 1779 she wrote an essay in support of better access to education for young women.

In 1786 John Stevens died in the West Indies, where he had fled to escape arrest for not paying his debts. Two years later, Judith Stevens married John Murray, the preacher at the Universalist Church she attended. After giving birth to two children, only one of whom lived beyond infancy, Judith Murray began to write again. Although she continued to write poetry, she began a series of essays published in the *Massachusetts Magazine* that today are considered her most famous works. The essays, each called "The Gleaner," are written from the point of view of a man named Mr. Vigilius. In these essays, Murray writes about religion, politics, education, and social manners. A frequent theme is appropriate parenting for girls and young women. Murray believed that a woman should be educated both for her own personal growth and to be a "sensible and informed" companion to a man. Murray also believed that a woman is capable of earning her own income.

In 1793 Murray's family moved to Boston, where she wrote her first play, *The Medium*. The play was not successful, and as a result the Murrays faced financial troubles. John Murray suggested that Judith collect her "Gleaner" essays into one publication. Today this collection, entitled *The Gleaner*, ranks as one of the classics of early American literature.

HRW material copyrighted under notice appearing earlier in this work.

When Murray's husband had a severe stroke in 1809, she spent most of her time caring for him until his death in 1815. Following her daughter's marriage to the son of a wealthy Mississippi planter in 1812, the family's impaired financial condition improved. After completing her last literary work—a biographical piece on the life and sermons of her late husband—Judith Sargent Murray moved to Natchez, Mississippi, to live with her daughter and son-in-law. She died in 1820 at the age of 69.

**UNDERSTANDING WHAT YOU READ**   After you have finished reading the selection, answer the following questions in the space provided.

**1.** How did Judith Sargent Murray receive much of her education during her teen years?

_____

_____

**2.** What kinds of writing did Murray do?

_____

_____

**3.** How did the American Revolution influence Murray's thoughts?

_____

_____

**4.** What topics were the focus of the series of essays called "The Gleaner"?

_____

_____

## ACTIVITY

Imagine that you are Judith Sargent Murray and that you are writing a newspaper advice column. On a separate sheet of paper, create a letter that a reader might send concerning the need for better education for girls, and write a response that reflects Murray's opinions.

HRW material copyrighted under notice appearing earlier in this work.

★ ★ ★ ★ ★ ★ ★ ★ ★ ★ ★ ★ ★ ★ ★ ★ ★ ★ ★ ★

# PRIMARY SOURCE READING

## Jefferson's Inaugural Address

*The following selection is from Thomas Jefferson's first inaugural address. Jefferson, the first president to be inaugurated in Washington, D.C., delivered this address on March 4, 1801, in the Senate Chamber—the only part of the Capitol then completed. Although Jefferson had opposed the Federalists for years, in his inaugural address he spoke of uniting Federalists and Republicans. As you read the speech, pay attention to the principles that Jefferson emphasizes.*

Let us then, fellow citizens, unite with one heart and one mind. . . .

We are all Republicans, we are all Federalists. If there be any among us who would wish to dissolve this Union or to change its republican form, let them stand undisturbed as monuments of the safety with which error of opinion may be tolerated where reason is left free to combat it. I know, indeed, that some honest men fear that a republican government cannot be strong, that this government is not strong enough. . . . I believe this, on the contrary, the strongest government on Earth. . . .

Let us, then, with courage and confidence pursue our own Federal and Republican principles, our attachment to union and representative government. . . .

Still one thing more, fellow citizens: a wise and frugal government, which shall restrain men from injuring one another, which shall leave them otherwise free to regulate their own pursuits of industry and improvement, and shall not take from the mouth of labor the bread it has earned. This is the sum of good government. . . .

You should understand what I deem [think] the essential principles of our government. . . .

Equal and exact justice to all men, of whatever state or persuasion [beliefs], religious or political; peace, commerce, and honest friendship with all nations, entangling alliances with none; the support of the state governments in all their rights; . . . a well-disciplined militia, our best reliance in peace and for the first moments of war till regulars may relieve them; . . . economy in the public expense that labor may be lightly burdened; the honest payment of our debts and sacred preservation of the public faith; encouragement of agriculture and of commerce as its handmaid; the diffusion [spread] of information; . . . freedom of religion, freedom of the press, and freedom of person under the protection of *habeas corpus*, and trial by juries impartially selected.

These principles form the bright constellation which has gone before us and guided our steps through an age of revolution and reformation. The

HRW material copyrighted under notice appearing earlier in this work.

wisdom of our sages [wise people] and blood of our heroes have been devoted to their attainment. They should be the creed [guiding principle] of our political faith.

**UNDERSTANDING WHAT YOU READ** After you have finished reading the selection, answer the following questions in the space provided.

**1.** Why does Jefferson believe that the U.S. government is the strongest government on Earth?

_____

_____

**2.** How does Jefferson define a "good government"?

_____

_____

**3.** What are some individual rights that Jefferson lists when discussing what he believes are the essential principles of government?

_____

_____

**4.** What are some of the principles that Jefferson lists to guide the actions of the federal government?

_____

_____

## ACTIVITY

Imagine that you are the president of the United States and are preparing to give your first inaugural address. On a separate sheet of paper, list some of the topics you would cover, what you would say about the government and the Constitution, and what you would share about your hopes for the future of the country.

HRW material copyrighted under notice appearing earlier in this work.

## The Expanding Nation

★ ★ ★ ★ ★ ★ ★ ★ ★ ★ ★ ★ ★ ★ ★ ★ ★ ★ ★ ★ ★ ★

## LITERATURE READING

# A Shawnee Leader Seeks Allies

*Tecumseh (1768–1813) was part of a Shawnee family that was committed to defending American Indian land and culture. His father and two brothers were killed in a battle with American colonists. A third brother, Tenskwatawa, was a holy man who led the Indians in a religious revival. Tecumseh, a great speaker and warrior, developed a military alliance among the Indian nations in the early years of U.S. independence. The following excerpt is from a speech he gave to the Osage while seeking allies in the Shawnee's fight to keep their land. As you read the selection, consider why Tecumseh wants the tribes to unite.*

Brothers—The white men are not friends to the Indians: at first, they only asked for land sufficient for a wigwam; now, nothing will satisfy them but the whole of our hunting grounds, from the rising to the setting sun.

Brothers—The white men want more than our hunting grounds; they wish to kill our warriors; they would even kill our old men, women, and little ones.

Brothers—Many winters ago, there was no land; the sun did not rise and set: all was darkness. The Great Spirit made all things. He gave the white people a home beyond the great waters. He supplied these grounds with game, and gave them to his red children; and he gave them strength and courage to defend them.

Brothers—My people wish for peace; the red men all wish for peace; but where the white people are, there is no peace for them, except it be on the bosom of our mother.

Brothers—The white men despise and cheat the Indians; they abuse and insult them; they do not think the red men sufficiently good to live.

The red men have borne many and great injuries; they ought to suffer them no longer. My people will not; they are determined on vengeance; they have taken up the tomahawk. . . .

Brothers—My people are brave and numerous; but the white people are too strong for them alone. I wish you to take up the tomahawk with them. . . .

Brothers—If you do not unite with us, they will first destroy us, and then you will fall an easy prey to them. They have destroyed many nations of red men because they were not united, because they were not friends to each other.

Brothers—The white people send runners amongst us; they wish to make us enemies, that they may sweep over and desolate [destroy] our hunting grounds, like devastating winds, or rushing waters.

HRW material copyrighted under notice appearing earlier in this work.

Brothers—Our Great Father over the great waters [the king of England] is angry with the white people, our enemies. He will send his brave warriors against them; he will send us rifles, and whatever else we want—he is our friend, and we are his children.

Brothers—Who are the white people that we should fear them? They cannot run fast, and are good marks to shoot at: they are only men; our fathers have killed many of them; we are not squaws, and we will stain the earth red with their blood.

Brothers—The Great Spirit is angry with our enemies; he speaks in thunder, and the earth swallows up villages, and drinks up the Mississippi. The great waters will cover their lowlands; their corn cannot grow; and the Great Spirit will sweep those who escape to the hills from the earth with his terrible breath.

Brothers—We must be united; we must smoke the same pipe; we must fight each other's battles; and more than all, we must love the Great Spirit; he is for us; he will destroy our enemies, and make his red children happy.

---

From *Memoirs of a Captivity Among the Indians of North America* by John D. Hunter. London, 1924.

**UNDERSTANDING WHAT YOU READ**   After you have finished reading the selection, answer the following questions in the space provided.

**1.** To whom is Tecumseh speaking?

_____

_____

**2.** What bad things does Tecumseh say that the white men are doing to the American Indians?

_____

_____

**3.** Why does Tecumseh ask the Osage to unite with his tribe, the Shawnee?

_____

_____

**4.** Why would the "Great Father over the great waters" want to help the American Indians fight against the colonists?

_____

_____

HRW material copyrighted under notice appearing earlier in this work.

**5.** According to Tecumseh, how does the Great Spirit feel about the white people?

_____

_____

## ACTIVITY

Imagine that you are a member of the Osage tribe who heard Tecumseh give this speech. On a separate sheet of paper, come up with a slogan that illustrates either support for or opposition to joining with the Shawnee.

HRW material copyrighted under notice appearing earlier in this work.

## CHAPTER 11

### The Expanding Nation

★ ★ ★ ★ ★ ★ ★ ★ ★ ★ ★ ★ ★ ★ ★ ★ ★ ★ ★ ★ ★ ★ ★

## BIOGRAPHY READING

# Sacagawea

*One of the more famous women of the American West is Sacagawea, the only woman who accompanied the Lewis and Clark expedition. A Shoshone, Sacagawea served as a guide and interpreter to the expedition. Her help proved essential to the expedition's success.*

Many details of Sacagawea's life are not well-known. Historians know, however, that she was born in a Shoshone village somewhere near modern-day Lemhi, Idaho, around 1787. In 1800 a war party of Hidatsas Indians captured Sacagawea and many others from her village. She was taken to a Hidatsas village near the mouth of the Knife River. There she and another girl were sold to a Canadian fur trapper named Toussaint Charbonneau, who married both women.

Meriwether Lewis and William Clark later hired Charbonneau to be the interpreter for their expedition. Sacagawea joined the expedition because she had come from territory near the Rocky Mountains and spoke both Shoshone and Minitari. In addition, Lewis and Clark believed that having a woman accompany them would indicate to other tribes that their mission was peaceful.

Sacagawea's services proved extremely valuable. When the expedition came to the main village of the Shoshone, Sacagawea worked as their interpreter. With her help the expedition hired a Shoshone guide and traded with the Indians for riding and pack horses. Happily, Sacagawea was reunited with her brother, Cameawhait, who was now chief of the Shoshone. Although Sacagawea may have been tempted to rejoin her family and her people, she decided to continue on with the expedition.

Although the expedition successfully reached the Pacific Ocean, President Thomas Jefferson—who had supported the exploration—was disappointed to find that there was not an easy route across the West. In return for their work, most members of the expedition were given grants of land. Sacagawea, however, was never compensated for her services.

The remaining years of Sacagawea's life were spent accompanying her husband as he sought his fortune. In 1812 the couple and their infant daughter joined a friend near the present-day North and South Dakota border. It is there that an account of Sacagawea's death was recorded. A clerk wrote that the wife of Charbonneau died of a very high fever, and that her infant daughter was taken to St. Louis and placed under the guardianship of William Clark. Although this has been the accepted account of her death, some people believe that Sacagawea returned to the Shoshone and lived among them until she was 100 years old. She is thought to be the woman known as "Bazil's Mother," who was buried in the Shoshone burial grounds in 1884.

HRW material copyrighted under notice appearing earlier in this work.

No other American woman has been honored with so many memorials. A river, a mountain peak, and a mountain pass have all been named after Sacagawea. There are two bronze statues—one in Portland, Oregon, and the other in Bismarck, North Dakota. A boulder is dedicated to her at Three Forks, Montana, as are a monument at Armstead, Montana, a public fountain in Lewiston, Idaho, and a cement shaft at her supposed grave on the Shoshone reservation.

**UNDERSTANDING WHAT YOU READ**    After you have finished reading the selection, answer the following questions in the space provided.

**1.** Which Native American tribe did Sacagawea belong to? Where did they live?

_____

_____

**2.** How did Sacagawea help the Lewis and Clark expedition? How was she rewarded for her services?

_____

_____

**3.** What are the two stories of Sacagawea's death? Why do you think there is more than one story about her death?

_____

_____

**4.** List some of the monuments that have been built to Sacagawea.

_____

_____

**ACTIVITY**

Imagine that your city has asked you to design a memorial to Sacagawea. Create a sketch of your memorial, and include a plaque that explains how your memorial reflects her contributions to U.S. history. You may want to search the Internet through the HRW Go site for examples of other memorials in the United States.

 go.hrw.com
**SA1 Monument**

HRW material copyrighted under notice appearing earlier in this work.

## A New National Identity

★ ★ ★ ★ ★ ★ ★ ★ ★ ★ ★ ★ ★ ★ ★ ★ ★ ★ ★ ★

# PRIMARY SOURCE READING

## The Trail of Tears

*On December 29, 1835, a small number of leaders from the Cherokee Nation signed the Treaty of New Echota, in which they agreed to give up their tribal homelands in Georgia and move to land west of the Mississippi River in exchange for $5 million. Only a few Cherokee supported the treaty; most remained in Georgia. In May 1838 President Martin Van Buren ordered General Winfield Scott to force the remaining Cherokee to move.*

*More than 4,000 people—almost a quarter of the Cherokee Nation—died during the journey to Indian Territory, many from disease and lack of shelter. Those who survived the journey, which came to be known as the "Trail of Tears," found life difficult once they arrived in Indian Territory. Following are observations of people who participated in or witnessed the Trail of Tears. As you read the excerpts, consider the conditions under which the Cherokee made this journey.*

When the soldier came to our house my father wanted to fight, but my mother told him that the soldiers would kill him if he did and we surrendered without a fight. They drove us out of our house to join other prisoners in a stockade [fortification]. After they took us away, my mother begged them to let her go back and get some bedding. So they let her go back and she brought what bedding and a few cooking utensils she could carry and had to leave behind all of our other household possessions.

My father had a wagon pulled by two spans [teams] of oxen to haul us in. Eight of my brothers and sisters and two or three widow women and children rode with us. My brother Dick, who was a good deal older than I was, walked along with a long whip which he popped over the backs of the oxen and drove them all the way. My mother and father walked all the way also.

The people got so tired of eating salt pork on the journey that my father would walk through the woods as we traveled, hunting for turkeys and deer which he brought into camp to feed us. Camp was usually made at some place where water was to be had and when we stopped and prepared to cook our food, other emigrants who had been driven from their homes without opportunity to secure cooking utensils came to our camp to use our pots and kettles. There was much sickness among the emigrants and a great many little children died of whooping cough.

—Rebecca Neugin, who made the journey at age three

HRW material copyrighted under notice appearing earlier in this work.

One can never forget the sadness and solemnity [seriousness] of that morning. . . .

I saw the helpless Cherokees arrested and dragged from their homes, and driven by bayonet into the stockades. And in the chill of a drizzling rain on an October morning I saw them loaded like cattle or sheep into six hundred and forty-five wagons and started toward the west. . . .

Chief Ross led in prayer and when the bugle sounded and the wagons started rolling many of the children . . . waved their little hands good-bye to their mountain homes.

—Private John Burnett

[We saw a] detachment of the poor Cherokee Indians . . . about eleven hundred Indians—sixty wagons—six hundred horses, and perhaps forty pairs of oxen. We found them in the forest camped for the night by the road side . . . under a severe fall of rain accompanied by heavy wind. With their canvas for a shield from the inclemency [harshness] of the weather, and the cold wet ground for a resting place, after the fatigue [tiredness] of the day, they spent the night. . . . Many of the aged Indians were suffering extremely from the fatigue of the journey, and the ill health consequent upon [resulting from] it. . . . Several then were quite ill, and an aged man, we were informed, was then in the last struggles of death. . . .

The sick and feeble were carried in waggons—about as comfortable for traveling as a New England ox cart with a covering over it—a great many ride on horseback and multitudes go on foot—even aged females, apparently nearly ready to drop into the grave, were traveling with heavy burdens attached to the back—on sometimes frozen ground, and sometimes muddy streets, with no covering for the feet except what nature had given them. . . . We learned from the inhabitants on the road where the Indians passed that they buried fourteen or fifteen at every stopping place, and they make a journey of ten miles per day only on an average.

—A traveler from Maine who had passed several Cherokee groups on the way west

---

From "Memories of the Trail" by Rebecca Neugin from *Indian Removal* by Grant Foreman. Published by the University of Oklahoma Press, 1932.

## UNDERSTANDING WHAT YOU READ   After you have finished reading the selection, answer the following questions in the space provided.

**1.** Describe the way that the soldiers collected the Cherokee for the journey.

_____

_____

HRW material copyrighted under notice appearing earlier in this work.

**2.** What modes of transportation were available to the Cherokee?

_____

_____

**3.** What were some of the items that the Cherokee were able to bring with them for the journey?

_____

_____

**4.** Why do you think that some of the Cherokee agreed to the Treaty of New Echota and others did not?

_____

_____

## ACTIVITY

Imagine that you are one of the U.S. soldiers assigned to move the Cherokee to the Indian Territory. On a separate sheet of paper, write a letter home to your family describing your duties, the conditions of the journey, and some of the events that occur along the way.

HRW material copyrighted under notice appearing earlier in this work.

# "Rip Van Winkle"

*Washington Irving was the first American writer to achieve an international literary reputation. Irving was born in New York City in 1783 and was the last of 11 children. He enjoyed reading English prose, modeled his initial writings in that style, and lived abroad in England for 18 years. While he completed many works about English life, he also wrote two stories set in rural New York that were distinctively American tales, "Rip Van Winkle" and "The Legend of Sleepy Hollow." These two stories concentrated on unique aspects of American life. Americans identified with the character of Rip Van Winkle, a type of counter-hero who made a success of failure. As you read the excerpt, consider how Irving shows the speed of change in American life.*

In that same village, and in one of these very houses . . . there lived many years since, while the country was yet a province of Great Britain, a simple good natured fellow, of the name of Rip Van Winkle. . . . Rip Van Winkle, however, was one of those happy mortals, of foolish, well-oiled dispositions [easy-going natures], who take the world easy, eat white bread or brown, which ever can be got with least thought or trouble, and would rather starve on a penny than work for a pound. If left to himself, he would have whistled life away, in perfect contentment; but his wife kept continually dinning [complaining] in his ears about his idleness, his carelessness, and the ruin he was bringing on his family. . . . Poor Rip was at last reduced almost to despair; and his only alternative to escape from the labour of the farm and the clamour of his wife, was to take gun in hand, and stroll away into the woods. . . .

In a long ramble of the kind on a fine autumnal [fall] day, Rip had unconsciously scrambled to one of the highest parts of the Kaatskill [Catskill] mountains. . . . As he was about to descend, he heard a voice from a distance, hallooing [calling], "Rip Van Winkle! Rip Van Winkle!" . . . On nearer approach, he was still more surprised at the singularity [unusual character] of the stranger's appearance. He was a short square built old fellow, with thick bushy hair, and a grizzled [grey-streaked] beard. . . . He bore on his shoulder a stout keg . . . and made signs for Rip to approach and assist him with the load. . . . New objects of wonder presented themselves. On a level spot in the center was a company of odd-looking personages playing at ninepins [bowling]. . . . By degrees, Rip's awe [wonder] and apprehension [nervousness] subsided [became less]. He even ventured . . . to taste the beverage. . . . One taste provoked another . . . that at length his senses were overpowered, his eyes swam in his head, his head gradually declined, and he fell into a deep sleep. . . .

On awaking, he found himself on the green knoll from whence he had first seen the old man of the glen. . . . "Surely," thought Rip, "I have not slept

HRW material copyrighted under notice appearing earlier in this work.

here all night." . . . As he approached the village, he met a number of people, but none that he knew. . . . Their dress, too, was of a different fashion . . . They all stared at him . . . to his astonishment, he found his beard had grown a foot long. . . . The very village seemed altered: it was larger and more populous. . . . Strange names were over the doors—strange faces at the windows—every thing was strange. . . .

The appearance of Rip, with his long grizzled beard, his rusty fowling piece [gun], his uncouth dress, and the army of women and children that had gathered at his heels, soon attracted the attention of the tavern politicians. They crowded around him, eyeing him from head to foot, with great curiosity. . . . The honest man could contain himself no longer . . . "Does nobody know poor Rip Van Winkle!" . . . All stood amazed, until an old woman . . . exclaimed "Sure enough! it is Rip Van Winkle . . . Why, where have you been these twenty long years?" Rip's story was soon told, for the whole twenty years had been to him but as one night. . . .

Rip's daughter took him home to live with her . . . It was some time before he could get into the regular track of gossip, or could be made to comprehend [understand] the strange events that had taken place . . . How that there had been a revolutionary war . . . and that, instead of being a subject of his Majesty George the Third, he was now a free citizen of the United States.

---

From *Rip Van Winkle* by Washington Irving in *The Norton Anthology of American Literature: Third Edition, Volume 1.* Copyright © 1989 by W. W. Norton & Company, Inc.

**UNDERSTANDING WHAT YOU READ**    After you have finished reading the selection, answer the following questions in the space provided.

**1.** How does Irving describe Rip Van Winkle?

_____

_____

**2.** Why does Rip go up into the mountains? Who does he meet there?

_____

_____

**3.** What causes Rip to fall asleep? What does he think when he wakes up?

_____

_____

HRW material copyrighted under notice appearing earlier in this work.

**4.** What convinces the villagers that Rip is who he says he is? How long has he really been gone?

_____

_____


**5.** What events has Rip missed while he has been asleep?

_____

_____


## ACTIVITY

Imagine that you accidentally fell asleep for 20 years and then suddenly awakened. On a separate sheet of paper, write a brief story describing what happens when you awake. You might describe how your town or city has changed, differences in people you once knew, events that have happened, or how technology has changed.

HRW material copyrighted under notice appearing earlier in this work.

**CHAPTER 12**

## A New National Identity

★ ★ ★ ★ ★ ★ ★ ★ ★ ★ ★ ★ ★ ★ ★ ★ ★ ★ ★ ★ ★ ★ ★ ★

## BIOGRAPHY READING

# Henry Clay

*Henry Clay was an American statesman and politician and one of the most popular and influential leaders in U.S. history. Especially known for his skills in the art of compromise, he helped resolve several major conflicts that threatened to tear the young nation apart. He was often referred to as the Great Pacificator.*

Henry Clay was born in 1777 in Virginia to a middle-class family. His father was a Baptist minister who died when Clay was only four years old. After attending public school and studying for the bar, Clay moved to Lexington, Kentucky, in 1797. There he established a successful criminal law practice. In 1799 he wed Lucretia Hart. The couple had 11 children.

Clay had a quick mind, a talent for public speaking, and the ability to charm almost everyone with his easy and attractive manner. It has been reported that no person was ever hanged in a trial where Clay appeared for the defense. He was elected to the Kentucky state legislature, where he served for six years. Clay served several terms in the U.S. House of Representatives between 1811 and 1825. During his first term in the House, he established a reputation as one of the leading War Hawks, a group that favored going to war with Great Britain. Clay was later selected as one of the commissioners to negotiate the Treaty of Ghent, which ended the War of 1812.

In 1820 and 1821 Clay played an important role in drafting the Missouri Compromise, which temporarily ended the conflict about the balance between slave states and free states. Although Clay was a slaveholder, he was able to gain support from people on both sides of the issue. In 1824 Clay made an unsuccessful bid for the presidency. When his campaign failed, he threw his support behind John Quincy Adams. President Adams then named Clay secretary of state.

Clay took a very strong view on what he called the "American System." He called for protectionist tariffs in support of manufacturing, internal improvements such as road and canal projects, a strong national bank, and the distribution of money from federal land sales to individual states. Clay was elected to the U.S. Senate in 1831, where he served until 1842. In 1833 he drew up a compromise that resolved a crisis brought on by South Carolina's attempt to nullify a tariff set by Congress.

Clay's reluctance to support the annexation of Texas cost him the 1844 presidential election. He was elected to the Senate in 1849. Many believe that his greatest service to the nation came in 1850, when he helped win acceptance of a compromise that temporarily ended the threat of civil war over the issue of slavery in the new territories. He warned the South not to

HRW material copyrighted under notice appearing earlier in this work.

secede, because he believed that no such right existed. Clay died in 1852 at the age of 75.

**UNDERSTANDING WHAT YOU READ**  After you have finished reading the selection, answer the following questions in the space provided.

**1.** In what way did Clay establish his reputation in the House of Representatives?

_____

_____

**2.** What were some of the items that Clay viewed as essential to the "American System"?

_____

_____

**3.** Why did Clay lose the 1844 presidential election?

_____

_____

**4.** What was Clay's opinion about secession?

_____

_____

## ACTIVITY

On a separate sheet of paper, write a proverb or a saying that incorporates some of the values and political sensibilities of Henry Clay. The proverb might discuss the art of compromise or point out the wisdom of negotiating. You may want to search the Internet through the HRW Go site for examples of proverbs.

 go.hrw.com
**SA1 Proverbs**

HRW material copyrighted under notice appearing earlier in this work.

# The Lowell Girls

*Workers in the Lowell textile mills primarily were young women. One of these young women was Lucy Larcom, who began working in the mills at age 11. Although she left the mill several times to return to school or to find work elsewhere, Larcom generally felt that her work at the Lowell mill taught her much about her own abilities and character. As you read the following excerpt, consider how Larcom adapted to the regulations of mill work.*

I went to my first day's work in the mill with a light heart. The novelty of it made it seem easy, and it really was not hard just to change the bobbins [thread holders] on the spinning-frames every three-quarters of an hour or so, with half a dozen other little girls who were doing the same thing. When I came back at night, the family began to pity me for my long, tiresome day's work, but I laughed and said, "Why, it is nothing but fun. It is just like play."

And for a while it was only a new amusement; I liked it better than going to school and "making believe" I was learning when I was not. And there was a great deal of fun mixed with it. We were not occupied more than half the time. The intervals were spent frolicking around the spinning-frames, teasing and talking to the older girls, or entertaining ourselves with games and stories in a corner, or exploring, with the overseer's permission, the mysteries of the carding-room, the dressing-room, and the weaving-room.

I never cared much for machinery. The buzzing and hissing of pulleys and rollers and spindles and flyers around me often grew tiresome. I could not see into their complications, or feel interested in them. But in a room below us we were sometimes allowed to peer in through a sort of blind door at the great waterwheel that carried the works of the whole mill. It was so huge that we could only watch a few of its spokes at a time, and part of its dripping rim, moving with a slow, measured strength through the darkness that shut it in. It impressed me with something of the awe which comes to us in thinking of the great Power which keeps the mechanism of the universe in motion. . . .

When I took my next three months at the grammar school, everything there was changed, and I too was changed. The teachers were kind and thorough in their instruction, and my mind seemed to have been ploughed up during that year of work, so that knowledge took root in it easily. It was a great delight to me to study, and at the end of the three months the master told me that I was prepared for the high school.

But alas! I could not go. The little money I could earn—one dollar a week, besides the price of my board—was needed in the family, and I must return to the mill. . . .

HRW material copyrighted under notice appearing earlier in this work.

I began to reflect upon life rather seriously for a girl of twelve or thirteen. What was I here for? What could I make of myself? . . .

At this time I had learned to do a spinner's work, and I obtained permission to tend some frames that stood directly in front of the river windows, with only them and the wall behind me, extending half the length of the mill. . . .

The printed regulations forbade us to bring books into the mill, so I made my windowseat into a small library of poetry, pasting its side all over with newspaper clippings. . . .

Some of the girls could not believe that the Bible was meant to be counted among the forbidden books. We all thought that the Scriptures had a right to go wherever we went, and that if we needed them anywhere, it was at our work. I evaded [avoided] the law by carrying some leaves from a torn Testament in my pocket. . . .

The last window in the row behind me was filled with flourishing houseplants—fragrant-leaved geraniums, the overseer's pets. . . . T[he] perfume and freshness tempted me there often. . . . On the whole, it was far from being a disagreeable place to stay in. The girls were bright looking and neat, and everything was kept clean and shining. The effect of the whole was rather attractive to strangers. . . .

Still, we did not call ourselves ladies. We did not forget that we were working girls, wearing coarse aprons suitable to our work, and that there was some danger of our becoming drudges. I know that sometimes the confinement of the mill became very wearisome to me. In the sweet June weather I would lean far out of the window, and try not to hear the unceasing [unending] clash of the sound inside. Looking away to the hills, my whole stifled being would cry out, "Oh, that I had wings!"

------------------------------------------------------------------

From *A New England Girlhood* by Lucy Larcom. Reprinted in *Ordinary Americans: U.S. History Through the Eyes of Everyday People,* edited by Linda R. Monk. Copyright © 1994.

**UNDERSTANDING WHAT YOU READ**   After you have finished reading the selection, answer the following questions in the space provided.

**1.** What was Lucy Larcom's first opinion of work at the mill?

_____

_____

**2.** Why was she so impressed by the waterwheel?

_____

_____

HRW material copyrighted under notice appearing earlier in this work.

**3.** How did Larcom get around the regulations about reading in the mill?

_____

_____

**4.** How did workers and mill owners try to create a pleasant workplace?

_____

_____

## ACTIVITY

Imagine that you have been hired to work in a textile mill and you have moved out of your home to live in a dormitory with other mill workers. Write a letter to a cousin describing your feelings at the end of your first day of work.

HRW material copyrighted under notice appearing earlier in this work.

★ ★ ★ ★ ★ ★ ★ ★ ★ ★ ★ ★ ★ ★ ★ ★ ★ ★ ★ ★ ★ ★ ★ ★

# LITERATURE READING

## Transportation in the United States

*Charles Dickens was an English novelist who was born in 1812 and died in 1870. Even though Dickens had little formal education, he worked as a reporter and eventually became a successful writer. Dickens first visited the United States in 1842 and published a book about his experiences that same year. The following excerpt is about Dickens's travels from Washington, D.C., to Richmond, Virginia. As you read the selection, consider the traveling conditions Dickens encounters.*

We were to proceed [move on] in the first instance by steamboat: and as it is usual to sleep on board, in consequence of the starting hour being [because the steamboat leaves at] four o'clock in the morning, we went down to where she lay, at that very uncomfortable time for such expeditions [trips] when slippers are most valuable, and a familiar bed, in the perspective of an hour or two, looks uncommonly pleasant. . . .

I go on board . . . open the door of the gentlemen's cabin; and walk in. . . . To my horror and amazement it is full of sleepers in every stage, shape, attitude, and variety of slumber: in the berths [sleeping section], on the chairs, on the floors, on the tables, and particularly round the stove. . . . I take another step forward, and slip upon the shining face of a black steward, who lies rolled in a blanket on the floor. He jumps up, grins, half in pain and half in hospitality. . . . I count these slumbering passengers, and get past forty. . . . I . . . go to sleep.

I wake, of course, when we get under way, for there is a good deal of noise. The day is then just breaking. Everybody wakes at the same time. . . . Some yawn, some groan, nearly all spit, and a few get up. I am among the risers. . . . Everybody uses the comb and brush, except myself. Everybody stares to see me using my own. . . .

At eight o'clock we breakfast in the cabin where I passed the night, but the windows and doors are all thrown open, and now it is fresh enough. . . .

Soon after nine o'clock we come to Potomac Creek, where we are to land: and then comes the oddest part of the journey. Seven stagecoaches are preparing to carry us on. . . . The passengers are getting out of the steamboat, and into the coaches; the luggage is being transferred in noisy wheelbarrows; the horses are frightened, and impatient to start; the . . . drivers are chattering to them . . . and . . . whooping like . . . drovers: for the main thing to be done, in all kinds of hostlering [horsework] here, is to make as much noise as possible. . . .

HRW material copyrighted under notice appearing earlier in this work.

The tickets we have received on board the steamboat are marked No. 1, so we belong to coach No. 1. I throw my coat on the box, and hoist my wife and her maid into the inside. It has only one step, and that being about a yard from the ground, is usually approached by a chair: when there is no chair, ladies trust in Providence. The coach holds nine inside, having a seat across from door to door, where we in England put our legs: so that there is only one feat more difficult in the performance than getting in, and that is getting out again. There is only one outside passenger, and he sits upon the box. As I am that one, I climb up; and . . . have a good opportunity of looking at the driver.

. . . He is dressed in a coarse pepper-and-salt suit excessively patched and darned (especially at the knees), grey stockings, enormous unblacked high-low shoes, and very short trousers. . . . [S]omebody in authority cries "Go ahead!" as I am making these observations. . . . [A]ll the coaches follow in procession.

By the way, whenever an Englishman would cry "All right!" an American cries "Go ahead!" which is somewhat expressive of the national character of the two countries.

------------------------------------------------------------

From *American Notes* by Charles Dickens. Copyright © 1985 by Granville Publishing. Reprinted by permission of St. Martin's Press.

**UNDERSTANDING WHAT YOU READ**  After you have finished reading the selection, answer the following questions in the space provided.

**1.** What time does the steamboat leave? What does Dickens think of this time?

_____

_____

**2.** Why is Dickens amazed when he enters the gentlemen's cabin?

_____

_____

**3.** How is Dickens awakened? What do the others do when they are awakened?

_____

_____

HRW material copyrighted under notice appearing earlier in this work.

**4.** Why does Dickens say that "All right!" and "Go ahead!" reflect the national characters of Great Britain and the United States, respectively?

_____

_____

## ACTIVITY

Imagine that you are a graphic artist working for the publisher of _American Notes_. On a separate sheet of paper, create a book cover that includes one of the scenes described above in the design.

HRW material copyrighted under notice appearing earlier in this work.

**CHAPTER**
**13**

## Industrial Growth in the North

★ ★ ★ ★ ★ ★ ★ ★ ★ ★ ★ ★ ★ ★ ★ ★ ★ ★ ★ ★ ★ ★ ★ ★

# BIOGRAPHY READING

# Robert Fulton

*Robert Fulton was an inventor, civil engineer, and artist who contributed to the industrial growth of the United States. He is often mistakenly named as the person who invented the steamboat; while Fulton did not invent it, he did design the first commercially successful steamboat in America, the* Clermont, *and has many other inventions to his credit.*

Robert Fulton was born in Lancaster County, Pennsylvania, in 1765. He was one of five children born to Robert and Mary Fulton. His father died when Robert was only three years old. Although she was left almost penniless, Mary Fulton kept the family together and tried to give her children a basic education. Fulton was sent to a private school when he was eight years old. Soon he began to show an exceptional talent for drawing and an aptitude for working with mechanical things. He studied the work of local gun makers and proved to be a competent gunsmith and gun designer. He also invented a type of paddle-wheel that he and his friends actually made use of on their fishing trips.

At the age of 17, Fulton went to Philadelphia to pursue a career in art. He was able to earn a living by creating portraits, mechanical drawings, and landscapes. He eventually made enough money to buy a farm for his family. Hard work and long hours eventually led to poor health, and he was advised to go abroad. In 1786 Fulton left for London to stay with a family friend named Benjamin West. He did not return to the United States for 20 years.

Although Fulton's first profession was painting, he became increasingly interested in engineering and formed friendships with some of the leading engineers of the time. After 1793 Fulton rarely painted, and never for money. He spent most of his time doing engineering projects for civil improvements, particularly to commercial waterways. He was especially interested in the development of canal systems, and invented a power shovel, or dredging machine, to cut channels. He also invented what he called a double inclined plane for raising and lowering canal boats. Fulton published his ideas about inland navigation in a series of essays, letters, and pamphlets. He believed that inland waterways would be the foundation of industry and transportation, and that economic and political expansion would depend on rivers and canals. He sent his writings on this topic to George Washington and to the governor of Pennsylvania.

In 1802 Fulton entered into an agreement with Robert R. Livingston to build a steamboat to travel the Hudson River between New York City and Albany. Livingston supplied the money and Fulton designed the experimental boat. Fulton launched his first steamboat in the spring of 1803. It broke apart and sank because it was not strong enough to support its steam

HRW material copyrighted under notice appearing earlier in this work.

engines. In August of that same year, Fulton tested an improved design that was used as the model for the steamboat to be built in New York.

In 1806 Fulton returned to New York to begin work on the *Clermont*. On August 17, 1807, the *Clermont* made its maiden voyage up the Hudson River. Fulton continued his involvement in steamboat production until his death in 1815.

**UNDERSTANDING WHAT YOU READ**   After you have finished reading the selection, answer the following questions in the space provided.

**1.** What were Fulton's early talents?

_____

_____

**2.** Why did Fulton believe that inland waterways were important?

_____

_____

**3.** What happened to the steamboat Fulton launched in the spring of 1803?

_____

_____

**4.** When was the first successful steamboat voyage made in America? On what body of water did the boat travel?

_____

_____

**ACTIVITY**

Imagine that you are a reporter who is writing an article about the successful voyage of the *Clermont*. Write a paragraph about the mood of people watching the steamboat as it travels up the Hudson River.

HRW material copyrighted under notice appearing earlier in this work.

## Agricultural Changes in the South

★ ★ ★ ★ ★ ★ ★ ★ ★ ★ ★ ★ ★ ★ ★ ★ ★ ★ ★ ★ ★ ★ ★ ★ ★

# PRIMARY SOURCE READING

## The Southern Economy

*John Rust Eaton was a landowner in the early 1800s with a sizable planta-tion in Granville County, North Carolina. He corresponded regularly with James Winchester, the owner of Cragfont, a large estate in Tennessee. In their letters, Eaton and Winchester frequently discussed politics and international events. As large landowners, they also had great interest in anything that affected trade, from the prices of cotton and tobacco to international events. Winchester also managed Eaton's plantation at Bartons Creek in Tennessee, and wrote to keep him informed of its status. As you read the letters, pay attention to Winchester's suggestions.*

CRAGFONT 3d Sep. 1806.

DEAR SIR

The General assembly of this State is now in session and is employed about a Land bill, which will probably pass into a law. it contemplates a Board of Commissions to decide on the Legality of all claims; it's therefore probable no warrants can be entered for sometime after the assembly rises [ends its session]; the land generally that was purchased of the Cherokee & Chickasaw Indians at the last Treaties is by no means equal to the land on Cumberland and Harpeth [rivers] besides . . . is not as convenient to naviga-tion Which in my opinion adds greatly to the value of [the] land. . . .

Cotton and Tobacco at present is the chief aim of all here who have any body to labour; the prices last year at [New] Orleans were flattering. Cotton from 20 to 24 cents lb. Tobacco 5 1/2 to 6 cents per lb.—If you have any Serious Thoughts of residing in this Country. I would recommend a purchase of land convenient to the navigation of [the] Cumberland river. and if your object is to realize for your Son; or Sons then purchase within the Indian boundary. . . .

This last Summer has been the wetest ever known in this country Since its first Settlement the crops are Generally very good But if the rains continue the Cotton will be injured—corn 125 cents Bll [per bushel]—

Remember me respectfully to your father and to Mrs. Eaton. and believe me It is my sincere wish to see them & you Citizens of Cumberland I already anticipate the pleasure of seeing you at my Cottage this fall, Make my respects to Mr. Smith and accept for Yourself the consideration

of my Esteem & regard

J. Winchester.

HRW material copyrighted under notice appearing earlier in this work.

CRAGFONT 14th April 1808

DEAR SIR

Your favor [letter] of the 22d of February came to hand in due time and ought to have been noticed sooner but a multiplicity of business in gloomy times since my return from the Northward must be my Apology. . . .

Your Bartons Creek plantation was last year rented for corn and is again this year my reason for doing so was; that I thought it possible you or some of your friends might change a sterile (as I have understood great parts of North Carolina to be) for a fertile spot and that it would be an object to have corn convenient, Cash it could not be rented for. . . .

Last years rent corn is not yet sold, nor will it bring one dollar cash per Barrel, Without advice on the subject I have thought it best to contract for no improvements on your plantation except the clearing a little land that was included within what had once been a fence. My reason is improvements are Seldom paid for in the Sale of Lands and if ever you occupy it yourself Such improvements as I could get made by a Tenant would not please you or even myself. . . .

Respectfully remember me to Mrs. Eaton tell her I still hope to have the pleasure to introduce her to my little family; uncultivated tho I hope innocent and for yourself accept

My sincere regard & Esteem

J. Winchester.

---

From *The James Sprunt Historical Publications*, edited by J. G. de Roulhac Hamilton. Published 1910 by the North Carolina Historical Society and the Commercial Printing Company.

**UNDERSTANDING WHAT YOU READ**   After you have finished reading the selection, answer the following questions in the space provided.

**1.** In James Winchester's 1806 letter, what did he have to say about cotton?

_____

_____

**2.** What problem did Winchester encounter concerning the rental of the Bartons Creek plantation?

_____

_____

**3.** Why did Winchester think Eaton might eventually move to his Bartons Creek plantation?

_____

_____

HRW material copyrighted under notice appearing earlier in this work.

**4.** Why was Winchester reluctant to authorize any improvements to Eaton's Bartons Creek plantation in 1808?

_____

_____

## ACTIVITY

Imagine that you are the author of an agricultural advice column in a southern newspaper. Using the information in these correspondences from Winchester to Eaton, compose a letter from a reader who seeks advice concerning which crop or crops to plant, and answer the letter with your sound advice.

HRW material copyrighted under notice appearing earlier in this work.

## Agricultural Changes in the South

★ ★ ★ ★ ★ ★ ★ ★ ★ ★ ★ ★ ★ ★ ★ ★ ★ ★ ★ ★ ★ ★

# LITERATURE READING

## *Incidents in the Life of a Slave Girl*

*During the 1800s, a new form of literature evolved: the slave narrative. As autobiographical accounts of the horrors of the slave system and their authors' quest for human dignity and freedom, slave narratives provided ammunition for the struggle to abolish slavery. Harriet A. Jacobs was one of the few black women to write a slave narrative. Born a slave in North Carolina around 1813, Jacobs went into hiding for years to escape an abusive master. She eventually fled to the North, where abolitionists helped her obtain her freedom.* Incidents in the Life of a Slave Girl *(1861) describes Jacobs's early life as a slave and the tension-filled relationships between blacks and whites under the slave system. As you read the excerpt, consider Jacobs's actions.*

Not far from this time Nat Turner's insurrection broke out[1]; and the news threw our town into great commotion. Strange that they should be alarmed, when their slaves were so "contented and happy"! But so it was.

It was always the custom to have a muster[2] every year. On that occasion every white man shouldered his musket. The citizens and the so-called country gentlemen wore military uniforms. The poor whites took their places in the ranks in every-day dress, some without shoes, some without hats. This grand occasion had already passed; and when the slaves were told there was to be another muster, they were surprised and rejoiced. Poor creatures! They thought it was going to be a holiday. I was informed of the true state of affairs, and imparted [told] it to the few I could trust. Most gladly would I have proclaimed it to every slave; but I dared not. All could not be relied on. Mighty is the power of the torturing lash.

By sunrise, people were pouring in from every quarter within twenty miles of the town. I knew the houses were to be searched; and I expected it would be done by country bullies and the poor whites. I knew nothing annoyed them so much as to see colored people living in comfort and respectability; so . . . I arranged every thing in my grandmother's house as neatly as possible. I put white quilts on the beds, and decorated some of the rooms with flowers. When all was arranged, I sat down at the window to watch. Far as my eye could reach, it rested on a motley [diverse] crowd of soldiers. Drums and fifes were discoursing [playing] martial [warlike] music. . . . Orders were given, and the wild scouts rushed in every direction, wherever a colored face was to be found.

-------------------------------------------------------------------------------
[1] Nat Turner's rebellion began August 21, 1831, in Southhampton County, Virginia, near Jacobs's owner's plantation.
[2] military inspection

HRW material copyrighted under notice appearing earlier in this work.

It was a grand opportunity for the low whites, who had no negroes of their own to scourge [punish]. They exulted in such a chance to exercise a little brief authority, and show their subserviency to the slaveholders; not reflecting that the power which trampled on the colored people also kept themselves in poverty, ignorance, and moral degradation. Those who never witnessed such scenes can hardly believe what I know was inflicted at this time on innocent men, women, and children, against whom there was not the slightest ground for suspicion. Colored people and slaves who lived in remote parts of the town suffered in an especial manner. In some cases the searchers scattered powder and shot among their clothes, and then sent other parties to find them, and bring them forward as proof that they were plotting insurrection. Every where men, women, and children were whipped till the blood stood in puddles at their feet. . . . The dwellings of the colored people, unless they happened to be protected by some influential [powerful] white person, who was nigh [near] at hand, were robbed of clothing and every thing else the marauders [attackers] thought worth carrying away. All day long these unfeeling wretches went round, like a troop of demons, terrifying and tormenting the helpless. At night, they formed themselves into patrol bands, and went wherever they chose among the colored people, acting out their brutal will. . . . The consternation [fear] was universal. No two people that had the slightest tinge of color in their faces dared to be seen talking together. . . .

The day patrol continued for some weeks, and at sundown a night guard was substituted. Nothing at all was proved against the colored people, bond or free. The wrath of the slaveholders was somewhat appeased [calmed] by the capture of Nat Turner. The imprisoned were released. . . . Visiting was strictly forbidden on the plantations. The slaves begged the privilege of again meeting at their little church in the woods. . . . Their request was denied, and the church was demolished. They were permitted to attend the white churches, a certain portion of the galleries [balconies] being appropriated to their use.

---

From Harriet A. Jacobs, *Incidents in the Life of a Slave Girl*. Harvard University Press, 1987.

## UNDERSTANDING WHAT YOU READ   After you have finished reading the selection, answer the following questions in the space provided.

**1.** Why do the townspeople hold a second muster?

_____

_____

**2.** Why is the searching of the houses done by the poorer whites of the community?

_____

_____

HRW material copyrighted under notice appearing earlier in this work.

**3.** What are some of the events that occur during the search?

_____

_____

**4.** What happens to the slaves' church?

_____

_____

**5.** Why do you think the author arranges her grandmother's house in such a neat and orderly manner?

_____

_____

## ACTIVITY

Imagine that you are someone living during this time period who believes in the abolition of slavery. On a separate sheet of paper, write a brief paragraph that uses examples from the reading to argue that the issue of slavery is about more than economic concerns.

HRW material copyrighted under notice appearing earlier in this work.

**CHAPTER 14**

## Agricultural Changes in the South

★ ★ ★ ★ ★ ★ ★ ★ ★ ★ ★ ★ ★ ★ ★ ★ ★ ★ ★ ★ ★ ★

## BIOGRAPHY READING

# Fanny Kemble

*Fanny Kemble was an English actress who married into a wealthy Georgia plantation family. As she was gradually exposed to the realities of life in the South under the slave system, she became convinced of the evils of slavery. Kemble later wrote an account of life on a southern plantation.*

Fanny Kemble was born Frances Anne Kemble on November 27, 1809, to Charles Kemble and Maria Theresa De Camp. Both Kemble and De Camp were actors, and their daughter was the niece of the two greatest British stage actors of the time—John Philip Kemble and Sarah Siddons. As a child, Fanny Kemble was sent to school in France. She returned to England at the age of 15 and in 1829 made her stage debut, playing Juliet in a family production of Shakespeare's *Romeo and Juliet*. She was an instant hit and was compared to her famous aunt. Her father brought her to the United States in 1832 to tour the nation. Kemble disliked some aspects of the theater and was looking for a new life. In 1834 Kemble accepted a marriage proposal from Pierce Butler, a wealthy Georgia plantation owner, and retired from the stage.

The Butler family did not approve of Kemble's career as an actress, nor of her abolitionist beliefs. After the birth of their two daughters, the Butlers moved to the Georgia plantation in 1838. Kemble was horrified at the living and working conditions of slaves. She tried to help the slaves any way she could, although her husband disapproved of this and was upset by her independence.

In 1846 Kemble left Georgia and returned to England alone. She took up acting again, in spite of her negative feelings toward it. Kemble would later turn to reading Shakespeare's work rather than acting it out. She returned to the United States in 1849 and purchased a home in Lenox, Massachusetts. Kemble continued to do Shakespearean readings throughout the 1850s and into the 1860s, and her performances met with great success.

When the Civil War broke out, Kemble supported the North because of her strong antislavery views. After returning to England in 1862, she decided to write a book in response to the Confederate sympathies of her British friends. In 1863 she published *Journal of a Residence on a Georgia Plantation*, an alarming account of her first impressions of slavery and the horrors and tragedies of the slave system.

Kemble moved back to the United States in 1867 and began working on her autobiography. A series of her essays ran in the *Atlantic Monthly* from 1879 to 1891 under the title "Old Woman's Gossip." In these writings Kemble recounted stories of the many important British and American people with whom she had crossed paths. This series brought Kemble a new audience. In

HRW material copyrighted under notice appearing earlier in this work.

1877 Fanny Kemble returned to London to be near her family and friends.
She died in 1893 at the age of 83.

**UNDERSTANDING WHAT YOU READ**   After you have finished reading the
selection, answer the following questions in the space provided.

**1.** Why did Kemble retire from stage in 1834?

_____

_____

**2.** Why did Kemble not get along with her husband and his family?

_____

_____

**3.** Why did Kemble write the *Journal of a Residence on a Georgia Plantation*?

_____

_____

**4.** What career did Kemble pursue after the Civil War?

_____

_____

**ACTIVITY**

Imagine that you have been hired to create a mural to depict the events in the
life of Fanny Kemble. Find a partner in your class and brainstorm ideas or
scenes for the mural. Then, on a separate sheet of paper, work together to
draw or sketch one scene from the mural.

HRW material copyrighted under notice appearing earlier in this work.

**CHAPTER 15**

## New Movements in America

★ ★ ★ ★ ★ ★ ★ ★ ★ ★ ★ ★ ★ ★ ★ ★ ★ ★ ★ ★ ★ ★ ★

# PRIMARY SOURCE READING

# "An Appeal to the Colored Citizens of the World"

*One of the most important events that helped trigger the antislavery crusade was the appearance in 1829 of "An Appeal to the Colored Citizens of the World" by David Walker. Walker was a freed slave living in Boston who believed that slavery was morally wrong and that the institution was degrading. Walker attacked the argument that African Americans were a different species that were not quite human and therefore not entitled to full rights under the Constitution. He also encouraged slaves to seize their own freedom at any cost. Although Walker died under mysterious circumstances, he was one of the strongest voices of the abolition movement. As you read the excerpt, pay attention to how Walker distinguishes American slaves from other oppressed people.*

My beloved brethren [brothers]:—The Indians of North and of South America—the Greeks—the Irish, subjected under the king of Great Britain—the Jews, that ancient people of the Lord—the inhabitants of the islands of the sea—in fine [in short], all the inhabitants of the earth, (except however, the sons of Africa) are called *men*, and of course are, and ought to be free. But we, (coloured people) and our children are *brutes!!* and of course are, and *ought to be* SLAVES to the American people and their children forever!! to dig their mines and work their farms; and thus go on enriching them, from one generation to another with our *blood* and our *tears!!!!*

I promised in a preceding [earlier] page to demonstrate to the satisfaction of the most incredulous [unbelieving], that we, (coloured people of these United States of America) are the *most wretched* [extremely bad], *degraded* and *abject* [lowly] set of beings that *ever lived* since the world began, and that the white Americans having reduced us to this wretched state of *slavery*, treat us in that condition *more cruel* (they being an enlightened and Christian people) than any heathen [non-Christian] nation did any people whom it had reduced to our condition. These affirmations [statements] are so well confirmed in the minds of all unprejudiced men, who have taken the trouble to read histories, that they need no elucidation [explanation] from me. . . .

I call upon the professing [people claiming to be] Christians, I call upon the philanthropist [donor], I call upon the very tyrant himself, to show me a page of history, either sacred or profane [not religious], on which a verse can be found, which maintains, that the Egyptians heaped the *insupportable* [unbearable] *insult* upon the children of Israel, by telling them that they were not of the *human family*. Can the whites deny this charge? Have they not, after having reduced us to the deplorable [very unfortunate] condition of slaves under their feet, held us up as descending originally from the tribes of

HRW material copyrighted under notice appearing earlier in this work

*Monkeys* or *Orang-Outangs*? O! my God! I appeal to every man of feeling—is not this insupportable? Is it not heaping the most gross [excessive] insult upon our miseries, because they have got us under their feet and we cannot help ourselves? . . . I do not know what to compare it to, unless, like putting one wild deer in an iron cage, where it will be secured, and hold another by the side of the same, then let it go, and expect the one in the cage to run as fast as the [other] one at liberty. . . .

Fear not the number and education of our *enemies*, against whom we shall have to contend for our lawful right; guaranteed to us by our Maker; for why should we be afraid, when God is, and will continue, (if we continue humble) to be on our side?

The man who would not fight under our Lord and Master Jesus Christ, in the glorious and heavenly cause of freedom and of God—to be delivered from the most wretched, abject and servile slavery, that ever a people was afflicted with [forced to suffer] since the foundation of the world, to the present day—ought to be kept with all of his children or family, in slavery, or in chains, to be butchered by his *cruel enemies*.

---

From David Walker's *Appeal, in Four Articles, together with a Preamble, to the Coloured Citizens of the World, but in Particular, and Very Expressly, to Those of the United States of America.* Copyright © 1965 by Hill and Wang, Inc.

**UNDERSTANDING WHAT YOU READ**   After you have finished reading the selection, answer the following questions in the space provided.

**1.** What does Walker say about the condition of African Americans in the United States?

_____

_____

**2.** What does Walker say is the "insupportable insult" that is being committed against African Americans?

_____

_____

**3.** Why does Walker state that white Americans are far worse and more hypocritical than any heathen nations that have had slaves?

_____

_____

HRW material copyrighted under notice appearing earlier in this work.

**4.** Who does Walker say is on the side of the African Americans? What should happen to the man who is not willing to fight for freedom?

_____

_____

**5.** What do you think that Walker means by the illustration of the deer in an iron cage?

_____

_____

## ACTIVITY

On a separate sheet of paper, draw a picture or a political cartoon illustrating the condition of the African Americans under slavery as compared to white Americans. For example, you might visually represent Walker's illustration of the deer in a cage.

HRW material copyrighted under notice appearing earlier in this work.

**CHAPTER 15**

## New Movements in America

★ ★ ★ ★ ★ ★ ★ ★ ★ ★ ★ ★ ★ ★ ★ ★ ★ ★ ★ ★ ★

## LITERATURE READING

# Encouraging Women's Rights

*Although sisters Sarah and Angelina Grimké were raised in the traditions of the South, they believed that slavery was morally wrong. After moving to the North, they gave public lectures supporting abolition. Both were criticized for "unladylike" behavior, which then encouraged them to speak out for women's rights. In her letters to Mary S. Parker, president of the Boston Female Antislavery Society, Sarah Grimké focused on the role white women should play in ending slavery. The letters also emphasize the importance of rights for women. As you read the selection, pay attention to Grimké's description of women's goals.*

Brookline, [Mass.] 1837.

My Dear Sister [Mary S. Parker],—

. . . During the early part of my life, my lot [fate] was cast among the butterflies of the *fashionable* world; and of this class of women, I am constrained [forced] to say, . . . that their education is miserably deficient [lacking]; that they are taught to regard marriage as the one thing needful, the only avenue to distinction [respect]; hence to attract the notice and win the attentions of men . . . is the chief business of fashionable girls. They seldom think that men will be allured [attracted] by intellectual acquirements, because they find, that where any mental superiority exists, a woman is generally shunned and regarded as stepping out of her "appropriate sphere," which, in their view, is to dress, to dance, to set out to the best possible advantage her person. . . . Fashionable women regard themselves, and are regarded by men, as pretty toys. . . .

There is another and much more numerous class in this country, who are withdrawn by education or circumstances from the circle of fashionable amusements, but who are brought up with the dangerous and absurd idea, that *marriage* is a kind of preferment; and that to be able to keep their husband's house, and render [make] his situation comfortable, is the end [only purpose] of her being. Much that she does and says and thinks is done in reference to this situation. . . . For this purpose more than any other, I verily [truly] believe the majority of girls are trained. . . . In most families, it is considered a matter of far more consequence to call a girl off from making a pie, or a pudding, than to interrupt her whilst engaged in her studies. . . .

Let no one think, from these remarks, that I regard a knowledge of housewifery as beneath the acquisition [learning] of women. Far from it: I believe that a complete knowledge of household affairs is an indispensable [completely necessary] requisite [requirement] in a woman's education. . . . All I complain of is, that our education consists so almost exclusively in culinary [cooking] and other manual operations. . . .

HRW material copyrighted under notice appearing earlier in this work.

The influence of women over the minds and character of *children* of both sexes, is allowed to be far greater than that of men. This being the case by the very ordering of nature, women should be prepared by education for the performance of their sacred duties as mothers and as sisters. . . .

There is another way in which the general opinion, that women are inferior to men, is manifested [made clear], that bears with tremendous effect on the laboring class, and indeed on almost all who are obliged to earn a subsistence [living], whether it be by mental or physical exertion—I allude [refer] to the disproportionate [very unequal] value set on the time and labor of men and of women. A man who is engaged in teaching, can always, I believe, command a higher price for tuition than a woman—even when he teaches the same branches [subjects], and is not in any respect superior to the woman. . . . A woman who goes out to wash, works as hard in proportion as a wood sawyer, or a coal heaver, but she is not generally able to make more than half as much by a day's work. . . .

There is another class of women in this country, to whom I cannot refer, without feelings of the deepest shame and sorrow. I allude to our female slaves. Our southern cities are whelmed [buried] beneath a tide of pollution; the virtue of female slaves is solely at the mercy of irresponsible tyrants. . . .

Can any American woman look at these scenes . . . and fold her hands in apathy [disinterest] and say, "I have nothing to do with slavery"? *She cannot and be guiltless.*

I cannot close this letter, without saying a few words on the benefits to be derived [experienced] by men, as well as women, from the opinions I advocate [support] relative to the equality of the sexes. Many women are now supported, in idleness and extravagance, by the industry of their husbands, fathers, or brothers, . . . while the wife and daughters and sisters take no part in the support of the family. . . . I believe that if women felt their responsibility, for the support of themselves, or their families it would add strength and dignity to their characters, and teach them more true sympathy. . . .


Thine in the bonds of womanhood,

Sarah M. Grimké

---------------------------------------------------------------

From Sarah Moore Grimké, *Letters on the Equality of the Sexes and the Condition of Woman, Addressed to Mary S. Parker, President of the Boston Female Anti-Slavery Society.* Reprinted in *Southern Women's Writing: Colonial to Contemporary.* Copyright © 1995 by the Board of Regents of the State of Florida.

HRW material copyrighted under notice appearing earlier in this work.

**UNDERSTANDING WHAT YOU READ**   After you have finished reading the
selection, answer the following questions in the space provided.

1. What does Grimké say is the goal of most young women in the United States?

   _____

   _____

2. What reason does Grimké give to support the need for educating women?

   _____

   _____

3. How does Grimké support her opinion that women are paid unfairly?

   _____

   _____

4. Why does Grimké feel that women should work to support themselves or their
   families?

   _____

   _____

**ACTIVITY**

Imagine that you are Sarah Grimké and you want to write a children's book
to teach young Americans about the need for women's equality. Create a
main character who encounters the different groups of women described in
this letter, and write a brief story that describes the character's experiences
and ideas. Be sure to include illustrations for your book.

HRW material copyrighted under notice appearing earlier in this work.

**New Movements in America**

★ ★ ★ ★ ★ ★ ★ ★ ★ ★ ★ ★ ★ ★ ★ ★ ★ ★ ★ ★ ★ ★ ★ ★

# BIOGRAPHY READING

# Mary Lyon

*Mary Lyon played a crucial role in the development of institutions of higher learning for women in America. Her passion for learning and education made her an excellent teacher and supporter of educational opportunities for all Americans. Her vision, drive, and determination led her to found Mount Holyoke, one of the first college-level schools for women in the United States.*

Mary Lyon was born to Aaron and Jemima Lyon on February 28, 1797, in Buckland, Massachusetts. Her father died before Mary reached the age of seven, and her mother had to take care of a large family with very little money. Hard work on the family farm did not dim Lyon's positive nature. She was intelligent and had a love of learning. It is reported that she mastered the principles of English grammar in four days, and Latin grammar in just three.

Lyon later attended both Ashfield and Amherst academies. In 1821 she attended the seminary at Byfield, a school that was famous because of its Reverend Joseph Emerson, a great supporter of women's education. Lyon's two terms at Byfield fueled her love of learning, and a commitment to teaching was born.

For the next 13 years, Lyon worked as a grammar and secondary school teacher. While teaching she was struck by the fact that there were no institutions of higher learning for women. She decided to establish a seminary. Lyon wanted a school where women from all social classes could receive an equal education. For the next six months, Lyon fought against indifference and opposition to her ideas.

On November 8, 1837, the Mount Holyoke Seminary opened in South Hadley, Massachusetts. Women entering the seminary were expected to have already been exposed to a quality education. The curriculum of the school was based on the subjects taught at Amherst College, including Latin, science, philosophy, and mathematics. In order to keep the tuition and living costs as low as possible, each student was assigned a particular household task.

The school became so popular that during the second year of its operation over 400 applicants were turned away for lack of room. The curriculum was expanded to include modern languages and music. Almost all of the instructors were female, with visiting lecturers from Amherst and Williams Colleges.

Mary Lyon died on March 5, 1849, at the age of 52. Her contribution to women's education was not only Mount Holyoke Seminary but also the educational theories on which the school's curriculum was based. She believed that education was intellectual, physical, and spiritual, and that a

HRW material copyrighted under notice appearing earlier in this work.

broad range of subjects helped to develop the individual. Mary Lyon also impressed upon her students that these educational opportunities should be used in the service of others.

**UNDERSTANDING WHAT YOU READ**    After you have finished reading the selection, answer the following questions in the space provided.

**1.** How did the young Mary Lyon demonstrate her intellectual abilities?

_____

_____

**2.** What was the original curriculum of Mount Holyoke Seminary? How was the curriculum expanded?

_____

_____

**3.** How did Mount Holyoke Seminary keep tuition and living costs as low as possible?

_____

_____

**4.** What educational theories did Mary Lyon develop?

_____

_____

**ACTIVITY**

Imagine that you are a student at Mount Holyoke. On a separate sheet of paper, create a journal entry that describes life at the school, the daily routine, and classes.

HRW material copyrighted under notice appearing earlier in this work.

CHAPTER
**16**

**Expanding West**

★ ★ ★ ★ ★ ★ ★ ★ ★ ★ ★ ★ ★ ★ ★ ★ ★ ★ ★ ★ ★ ★ ★ ★ ★

# PRIMARY SOURCE READING

## The Road to Oregon

*In the 1870s Jesse Applegate wrote a memoir describing his journey from Missouri to Oregon in 1843. The journey to Oregon was filled with hardships. As you read the selection, consider how Applegate views Americans.*

In the year 1843, the migration of a large body [group] of men, women, and children across the continent to Oregon was strictly an experiment in regard to both numbers of people and animals involved and the equipment of the migrating party. Before that date, two or three missionaries had made the journey on horseback, and three or four wagons drawn by oxen had reached Fort Hall on the Snake River [north of Utah's Great Salt Lake]. It was the honest opinion of those who had traveled down the Snake River that a large number of cattle could not subsist [survive] on the scanty pasture available; nor could wagons be taken on so rugged and mountainous a route. The emigrants were also assured that the Sioux probably would resist the passage of so large a body through their country, because of the emigrants destroying and frightening away the buffalo.

The migrating body numbered over 1,000 souls, with about 120 wagons, drawn by six-ox teams, and several thousand loose horses and cattle. The emigrants first attempted to travel in one body. But it was soon discovered that no progress could be made with so cumbersome [large and awkward] and undisciplined a body. After crossing "Big Blue" [River], the party divided into two columns. These traveled in supporting distance of each other as far as Independence Rock on the Sweetwater River [the beginning of the Rocky Mountains]. From this point, since all danger from Indians was over, the emigrants separated into smaller parties better suited to the narrow mountain paths and small pastures before them.

Not far from the beautiful scenery of Chimney Rock, we reached the top of a bluff and turned to view the wonderful panorama [view] spread before us. To those who have not been on the Platte, my powers of description are wholy inadequate to convey the vast extent and grandeur of the picture.

That picture, however, in its grandeur, . . . is forgotten in contemplation of the American people who give it life and animation. Only they would undertake so great a journey. . . .

They have undertaken, with slow-moving oxen, a journey of 2,000 miles. The way lies over trackless [unmarked] wastes, wide and deep rivers, rugged and lofty mountains, and is beset with hostile Indians. Yet, whether it is a deep river, a rugged gorge, . . . or a threatened attack from an enemy, they always are found equal to the occasion and always are conquerors. May we not call them people of destiny?

HRW material copyrighted under notice appearing earlier in this work

Here, I would like to pay tribute to that noble and devoted man, Dr. [Marcus] Whitman. From the time he joined us on the Platte until he left us at Fort Hall, his great experience and indomitable [unending] energy were of priceless value. His constant advice was "travel, *travel*, TRAVEL,—nothing else will take you to the end of your journey. Nothing is wise that does not help you along. Nothing is good that causes a moment's delay." It is no disparagement [insult] to others to say that the emigrants of 1843 are indebted to no one as much as they are to Dr. Marcus Whitman.

---

Adapted from "A Day with the Cow Column in 1843" by Jesse Applegate in *Oregon Historical Quarterly*, Vol. 1 (December, 1900). Reprinted in *Voices of America: Readings in American History*. Copyright © 1985 by Houghton Mifflin Company.

## UNDERSTANDING WHAT YOU READ   After you have finished reading the selection, answer the following questions in the space provided.

**1.** Why does Applegate describe the journey as an "experiment"?

_____

_____

**2.** Why did the party decide not to travel down the Snake River?

_____

_____

**3.** Why did the traveling party divide into two large groups until they had reached the Rocky Mountains?

_____

_____

**4.** What opinion does Applegate seem to have of Americans?

_____

_____

## ACTIVITY

Imagine that you are a member of the traveling party described by Applegate. Draw a picture that shows what the trip was like. For sample pictures of the region, you may wish to search the Internet through the HRW Go site.

  go.hrw.com

**SA1 Rocky Mountains**

HRW material copyrighted under notice appearing earlier in this work.

## Expanding West

★ ★ ★ ★ ★ ★ ★ ★ ★ ★ ★ ★ ★ ★ ★ ★ ★ ★ ★ ★ ★ ★

# LITERATURE READING

## On a California Ranch

*Folktales are stories that are passed from one generation to another by word of mouth. The folktale below tells something about Mexican American culture and about life on a ranch. As you read the selection, pay attention to Chicoria's behavior.*

There were once many big ranches in California, and many New Mexicans went to work there. One day one of the big ranch owners asked his workers if there were any poets in New Mexico.

"Of course, we have many fine poets," they replied. "We have old Vilmas, Chicoria, Cinfuegos, to say nothing of the poets of Cebolleta and the Black Poet."

"Well, when you return next season, why don't you bring one of your poets to compete with Gracia—here none can compare with him!"

When the harvest was done the New Mexicans returned home. The following season when they returned to California they took with them the poet Chicoria, knowing well that in spinning a rhyme or in weaving wit there was no *Californio* who could beat him.

As soon as the rancher found out that the workers had brought Chicoria with them, he sent his servant to invite his good neighbor and friend to come and hear the new poet. Meanwhile, the cooks set about preparing a big meal. When the maids began to dish up the plates of food, Chicoria turned to one of the servers and said, "Ah, my friends, it looks like they are going to feed us well tonight!"

The servant was surprised. "No, my friend," he explained, "the food is for *them.* We don't eat at the master's table. It is not permitted. We eat in the kitchen."

"Well, I'll bet I can sit down and eat with them," Chicoria boasted.

"If you beg or if you ask, perhaps, but if you don't ask they won't invite you," replied the servant.

"I never beg," the New Mexican answered. "The master will invite me of his own accord, and I'll bet you twenty dollars he will!"

So they made a twenty dollar bet and they instructed the serving maid to watch if this self-confident New Mexican had to ask the master for a place at the table. Then the maid took Chicoria into the dining room. Chicoria greeted the rancher cordially, but the rancher appeared haughty and did not invite Chicoria to sit with him and his guest at the table. Instead, he asked that a chair be brought and placed by the wall where Chicoria was to sit. The rich ranchers began to eat without inviting Chicoria.

So it is just as the servant predicted, Chicoria thought. The poor are not invited to share the rich man's food!

Then the master spoke: "Tell us about the country where you live. What are some of the customs of New Mexico?"

"Well, in New Mexico when a family sits down to eat each member uses

HRW material copyrighted under notice appearing earlier in this work.

one spoon for each biteful of food," Chicoria said with a twinkle in his eyes.

The ranchers were amazed that the New Mexicans ate in that manner, but what Chicoria hadn't told them was that each spoon was a piece of tortilla: one fold and it became a spoon with which to scoop up the meal.

"Furthermore," he continued, "our goats are not like yours."

"How are they different?" the rancher asked.

"Here your nannies give birth to two kids, in New Mexico they give birth to three!"

"What a strange thing!" the master said. "But tell us, how can the female nurse three kids?"

"Well, they do it exactly as you're doing it now: While two of them are eating the third one looks on."

The rancher then realized his lack of manners and took Chicoria's hint. He apologized and invited his New Mexican guest to dine at the table. After dinner, Chicoria sang and recited his poetry, putting Gracia to shame. And he won his bet as well.

---

"On a California Ranch" from *Cuentos: Tales from the Hispanic Southwest*, selected and adapted in Spanish by José Griego y Maestas, retold in English by Rudolfo A. Anaya. Copyright © 1980 by **The Museum of New Mexico Press**. Reprinted by permission of the publisher.

**UNDERSTANDING WHAT YOU READ**   After you have finished reading the selection, answer the following questions in the space provided.

**1.** What does the big ranch owner challenge the New Mexican workers to do?

_____

_____

**2.** How do the rich ranchers treat Chicoria at first?

_____

_____

**3.** How does Chicoria make the ranch owner realize that he is not being a very good host?

_____

_____

**ACTIVITY**

Imagine that you are a reporter writing a newspaper story about the events of this folktale. On a separate sheet of paper, record some possible newspaper headlines that would describe the events.

HRW material copyrighted under notice appearing earlier in this work.

★ ★ ★ ★ ★ ★ ★ ★ ★ ★ ★ ★ ★ ★ ★ ★ ★ ★ ★ ★ ★ ★ ★ ★ ★

## BIOGRAPHY READING

# Stephen F. Austin

*Many people call Stephen F. Austin the Founding Father of Texas. He was one of the first people to bring settlers into the state and was largely responsible for creating Texas's judicial system. The growth of the state was due largely to Austin's good relations with the Mexican government.*

Stephen Fuller Austin was born to Moses and Maria Austin on November 3, 1793. In 1798 the family moved to a lead-mining site in southeastern Missouri and established the town of Potosi. Austin lived there until the age of 10, when his father sent him to school in Connecticut. Austin later spent two years at Transylvania University in Kentucky. In 1810 he returned home to help his father in his lead business and general store. After the family business failed, he moved to Arkansas to work in real estate. By 1820 Austin was living in New Orleans, Louisiana, intending to study law.

Around the same time, Moses Austin traveled to San Antonio, Texas, to apply for a land grant and permission to settle 300 families in the area. Stephen Austin arranged for a loan to start the venture. When Moses Austin died, Stephen Austin continued his father's dream. He traveled to San Antonio, where he met with the Spanish governor of the area and gained permission to settle colonists in the area of the Texas coastal plain.

Austin's venture got off to a rocky start. In 1821 the Mexican government refused to recognize the Spanish land grant given to Moses Austin. Stephen Austin traveled to Mexico City to plead his case before the new government. In 1825 the legislature passed a law governing the settlement of colonists in the area and making special provisions for agents like Austin.

For the next several years, Austin helped American colonists settle in Texas. When disagreements arose between the colonists and the Mexican government, Austin tried to work out compromises. He also encouraged economic development, established schools, and was largely responsible for a law that allowed slaves to be brought to the state. By 1832 there were some 8,000 American residents living in Texas.

In 1832 Austin supported Antonio López de Santa Anna in his effort to overturn the central government. Austin participated in a movement to establish a separate state government in Texas at the Convention of 1833. The members chose him to deliver their petitions to the Mexican government in Mexico City. Austin was not successful, and on his way back to Texas he was arrested. He spent more than a year in Mexican prisons.

Austin was drawn into the Texas Revolution upon his return to Texas in 1835. After Texas won its independence from Mexico, Austin ran for president of the state but lost to Sam Houston. Houston then appointed Austin secretary of state, where he served until his death in 1836.

HRW material copyrighted under notice appearing earlier in this work.

**UNDERSTANDING WHAT YOU READ**   After you have finished reading the selection, answer the following questions in the space provided.

**1.** Why did Stephen F. Austin move to Texas?

_____

_____

**2.** Why did Austin's land venture get off to a rocky start? How did he resolve this problem?

_____

_____

**3.** What did Austin do when disagreements arose between the colonists and the Mexican government?

_____

_____

**4.** What happened when Austin went to Mexico City on behalf of the Convention of 1833?

_____

_____

**ACTIVITY**

Imagine that you are Stephen F. Austin and have just been put in prison. On a separate sheet of paper, write a letter to the president of Mexico explaining why you should be released.

HRW material copyrighted under notice appearing earlier in this work.

**CHAPTER 17**

## Manifest Destiny and War

★ ★ ★ ★ ★ ★ ★ ★ ★ ★ ★ ★ ★ ★ ★ ★ ★ ★ ★ ★ ★ ★ ★

## PRIMARY SOURCE READING

# Opposition to the Mexican War

*Although support for the Mexican War of 1846 was strong in some areas of the United States, voices against the war were also significant. Some argued that the invasion of another civilized country was against the spirit of freedom on which the Constitution and the nation were founded. One of the issues surrounding the war with Mexico was the annexation of territories such as Texas; some people, particularly abolitionists, feared the increase in the number of states allowing slavery. As you read these excerpts, pay attention to the connections drawn between slavery and war.*

In the total absence of any argument that can justify the war in which we are now involved, resort has been [made] to a most extraordinary assertion [claim]. It is said that the people of the United States have a hereditary superiority of race over the Mexicans, which gives them the right to subjugate [oppress] and keep in bondage the inferior nation. This, it is also alleged [claimed], will be the means of enlightening [educating] the degraded Mexicans, of improving their social state, and of ultimately increasing the happiness of the masses.

But admitting, with respect to Mexico, the superiority of race, this confers [gives] no superiority of rights. Among ourselves the most ignorant, the most inferior, either in physical or mental faculties [abilities], is recognized as having equal rights, and he has an equal vote with anyone, however superior to him in all those respects. This is founded on the immutable [unchangeable] principle that no man is born with the right of governing another man. . . .

The same principle will apply to nations. . . . The people of the United States may rightfully, and will, if they use the proper means exercise a most beneficial [helpful] moral influence over the Mexicans and other less enlightened nations of America. Beyond this they have no right to go.

—Albert Gallatin
*Peace with Mexico*, 1847

A war of conquest is bad; but the present war has darker shadows. It is a war for the extension of slavery over a territory which has already been purged [ridden] by Mexican authority from this stain and curse. Fresh markets of human beings are to be established; further opportunities for this hateful traffic are to be opened; the lash of the overseer is to be quickened in new regions; and the wretched slave is to be hurried to unaccustomed fields of toil.

—Charles Sumner
from "Report on the War with Mexico," 1847

HRW material copyrighted under notice appearing earlier in this work.

I never could see much good to come of annexation [of Texas]; inasmuch, as they were already a free republican people on our own model; on the other hand, I never could very clearly see how the annexation would augment [increase] the evil of slavery. It always seemed to me that slaves would be taken there in about equal numbers, with or without annexation. . . . I hold it to be a . . . duty of us in the free states, due to the Union of the states, and perhaps to liberty itself . . . to let the slavery of the other states alone; while, on the other hand, I hold it to be equally clear, that we should never . . . prevent that slavery from dying a natural death—to find new places for it to live in, when it can no longer exist in the old. . . .

— Abraham Lincoln

from a letter to Williamson Durley, 1845

In our judgment, those who have all along been loudly in favor of . . . the war . . . and glorifying the atrocious [horrible] deeds of barbarous heroism on the part of wicked men engaged in it, have no sincere love of . . . *peace* but *plunder* [stealing]. They have succeeded in robbing Mexico of her territory, and are rejoicing over their success under the hypocritical pretense [claim] of a regard for peace. . . . That an end is put to the wholesale murder in Mexico is truly just cause for rejoicing; but we are not the people to rejoice; we ought rather blush and hang our heads for shame, and . . . crave pardon for our crimes at the hands of a God whose mercy endureth [lasts] forever.

— Frederick Douglass

*The North Star*, March 17, 1848

**UNDERSTANDING WHAT YOU READ**  After you have finished reading the selection, answer the following questions in the space provided.

1. What does Albert Gallatin say is the "extraordinary assertion" that some people were using to justify the war with Mexico?

_____

_____

2. How did Abraham Lincoln think the annexation of Texas would affect slavery in Texas?

_____

_____

3. How does Frederick Douglass feel about the war with Mexico? What does he think the war is truly about?

_____

_____

HRW material copyrighted under notice appearing earlier in this work.

**4.** Charles Sumner claims that the war is about the extension of what institution?

_____

_____

**5.** What is Abraham Lincoln's attitude toward slavery in the United States?

_____

_____

## ACTIVITY

Imagine that you have to create a one-act play based on some of the arguments of people opposed to the Mexican War of 1846. On a separate sheet of paper, think about the elements you would include in your play, such as dialogue, characters, plot, and stage directions.

HRW material copyrighted under notice appearing earlier in this work

★ ★ ★ ★ ★ ★ ★ ★ ★ ★ ★ ★ ★ ★ ★ ★ ★ ★ ★ ★ ★ ★

# LITERATURE READING

## *The Squatter and the Don*

*In 1880 María Amparo Ruiz de Burton began writing the novel* The Squatter
and the Don. *Born in 1832 to a wealthy Californio family, she was well posi-
tioned to write about the Californios and their struggle to protect their land
against American squatters. In the novel Doña Josefa asks, "Is it possible that
there is no law to protect us; . . . is there no hope?" As you read her husband's
response, consider the problems of the Californios.*

"I remember," calmly said Don Mariano, "that when I first read the text of
the treaty of Guadalupe Hidalgo, I felt a bitter resentment against my people;
against Mexico, the mother country, who abandoned us—her children—with
so slight a provision of obligatory stipulations [necessary requirements] for
protection. But afterwards, upon mature reflection, I saw that Mexico did as
much as could have been reasonably expected at the time. In the very preamble of the treaty the spirit of peace and friendship, which animated both
nations, was carefully made manifest [clear]. That spirit was to be the *foundation* of the relations between the conqueror and the conquered. How could
Mexico have foreseen then that when scarcely half a dozen years should have
elapsed the trusted conquerors would, '*In Congress Assembled*,' pass laws
which were to be retroactive upon [taking away privileges already granted
to] the defenseless, helpless, conquered people, in order to despoil [ruin]
them? The treaty said that our rights would be the same as those enjoyed by
all other American citizens. But, you see, Congress takes very good care not
to enact retroactive laws for Americans; laws to take away from American
citizens the property which they hold now, already, with a recognized legal
title. No, indeed. But they do so quickly enough with us—with us, the Spano-
Americans, who were to enjoy equal rights, mind you, according to the treaty
of peace. This is what seems to me a breach [breaking] of faith, which Mexico
could neither presuppose [expect] nor prevent." . . .

[Don Mariano:] "We have had no one to speak for us. By the treaty of
Guadalupe Hidalgo the American nation pledged its honor to respect our
land titles just the same as Mexico would have done. Unfortunately, however,
the discovery of gold brought to California the riff-raff of the world, and with
it a horde [group] of land-sharks, all possessing the privilege of voting, and
most of them coveting [wanting] our lands, for which they very quickly began
to clamor [shout]. There was, and still is, plenty of good government land,
which any one can take. But no. The forbidden fruit is the sweetest. They do
not want government land. They want the land of the Spanish people,
because we 'have too much,' they say. So, to win their votes, the votes of the

HRW material copyrighted under notice appearing earlier in this work.

squatters, our representatives in Congress helped to pass laws declaring all lands in California open."

---

From *The Squatter and the Don* by María Amparo Ruiz de Burton, edited by Rosaura Sánchez and Beatrice Pita. Copyright © 1992 by Arte Público Press. Reprinted by permission *of Arte Público Press—University of Houston*.

## UNDERSTANDING WHAT YOU READ   After you have finished reading the selection, answer the following questions in the space provided.

**1.** How does Don Mariano describe his initial reaction to the Treaty of Guadalupe Hidalgo?

_____

_____

**2.** What type of laws does Don Mariano say are used against the Californios?

_____

_____

**3.** Why do such laws violate the spirit of the Treaty of Guadalupe Hidalgo?

_____

_____

**4.** What event has brought turmoil over the ownership of land to California?

_____

_____

**5.** What proverb does Don Mariano use to explain the actions of the squatters in California? What do you think he means by his statement?

_____

_____

## ACTIVITY

Imagine that you are a representative in Congress who is listening to a debate about the passage of the law that will declare all land in California "open" for settlement purposes. Based on what you know about the Treaty of Guadalupe Hidalgo and the rights it guaranteed to Californios, write a paragraph containing an argument you might make against the passage of the law.

HRW material copyrighted under notice appearing earlier in this work.

**CHAPTER 17**

## Manifest Destiny and War

★ ★ ★ ★ ★ ★ ★ ★ ★ ★ ★ ★ ★ ★ ★ ★ ★ ★ ★ ★ ★ ★

## BIOGRAPHY READING

# Brigham Young

*Brigham Young was the second president of the Mormon Church. He delivered more than 500 sermons during the 33 years he served as president. Young also colonized Utah and served as the state's first governor. He was a leading colonizer of the West and maintained friendly relations with American Indians.*

Brigham Young was born on June 1, 1801, to John and Abigail Young. The family moved to western New York when Young was three. Shortly after his mother died in 1815, Young left home and earned his living as a painter, handyman, and farmer. In 1824 he married Miriam Angeline Works. The couple settled in Monroe County, New York.

Young soon began to show a strong interest in religion. After Joseph Smith published the Book of Mormon in 1830, Young obtained a copy and began studying it carefully. He was baptized in the Church of Jesus Christ of Latter-Day Saints—the Mormon Church—in 1832. Young's baptism marked the beginning of his lifelong task in building the Mormon Church. He led a group of converts to Kirtland, Ohio, where he began his missionary work. Young was ordained an apostle in 1835 and became one of the Quorum of the Twelve—a group that directed missionary work, emigration and settlement, and construction projects. In 1838 Young directed the movement of Mormons from Missouri to Illinois.

In 1839 the Mormon Church sent Young to England on a missionary assignment. When he returned in 1841, he became the leading financial officer of the church. After Joseph Smith was murdered in July 1844, Young took command of the church. He gave it a new sense of direction and secured the loyalty of other church leaders.

As the new head of the Mormon Church, Young's ideas began to come into conflict with mainstream American society. Many people did not agree with the church's beliefs or practices. Young soon realized that the Mormon Church could not survive in the American social system and directed the migration of 16,000 Mormons from Illinois to Utah. It is not really known why Young chose the Great Salt Lake Valley in what is now Utah. Some historians believe that he acted on the assumption that his people could remain isolated and undisturbed in a desert location. Young might also have hoped that the physical isolation would strengthen the bond between the church and the community.

Young would later establish the Perpetual Emigrating Fund Company, which helped some 80,000 Mormon converts migrate to Utah from Europe. Many converts were tenant farmers or unemployed people in the cities who came for the promise of land as well as eternal salvation. Young also directed

HRW material copyrighted under notice appearing earlier in this work.

the colonization and development of some 350 settlements in Utah, Idaho, Wyoming, Nevada, Arizona, and California.

In 1851 Young contracted to build the transcontinental telegraph line from Nebraska to California. When Utah became a territory that same year, Young served as its first governor and superintendent of Indian affairs. As president of the Mormon Church, Young oversaw the construction of the Mormon Tabernacle in Salt Lake City and began the erection of the Salt Lake Temple. He also founded Brigham Young University and what would later become the University of Utah.

**UNDERSTANDING WHAT YOU READ**   After you have finished reading the selection, answer the following questions in the space provided.

**1.** How did Brigham Young become involved in the Mormon religion?

_____

_____

**2.** What events led Young to become the leader of the Mormon Church?

_____

_____

**3.** What problems did many people have with the Mormon Church?

_____

_____

**4.** Why do some historians think that Young chose Utah for the Mormon settlement?

_____

_____

**ACTIVITY**

Imagine that you are recording the physical movements of the Mormon Church. On a separate sheet of paper, create a map showing the journey of the church from its beginning in New York to its final destination in Utah.

HRW material copyrighted under notice appearing earlier in this work.

★ ★ ★ ★ ★ ★ ★ ★ ★ ★ ★ ★ ★ ★ ★ ★ ★ ★ ★ ★ ★ ★ ★ ★

# PRIMARY SOURCE READING

# A Response to the Fugitive Slave Act

*The passage of the Fugitive Slave Act dismayed abolitionists throughout the*
*United States. Government support of the arrest and return of escaped slaves*
*caused many abolitionists to re-evaluate their opinion of the nation's political*
*principles. In 1850 William P. Newman, a Baptist clergyman and former*
*slave, wrote to Frederick Douglass at the abolitionist newspaper the* North
Star. *In the excerpt below, Newman criticizes the federal government and*
*abandons his belief in pacifism, or the refusal to accept violence as a solution*
*to problems. As you read the selection, think about how Newman thought*
*people should react to the new law.*

CLEVELAND, O[hio]
Oct[ober] 1, 1850

FREDERICK DOUGLASS:

It seems to me that the world has misunderstood, till the sitting of the last
United States Congress, what the real and true mission of that government is.
Is it not a mission of bonds and death? Our race has been taught to think that
it was to be the example of all coming human governments, it being itself the
model of heaven. . . . But all must confess, that were all legislative governments to follow the example it has set of late, that earth would be anything
else than human.

   It may properly be asked, would not the Devil do well to *rent out hell*
and move to the United States, and rival, if possible, President Fillmore and
his political followers? . . . Would not fallen angels make wise and humane
Senators, compared with Cass, Clay and Webster? . . . The world must be
convinced that damned spirits would do better and honor more the representative hall. . . .

   Fillmore's heartless position, indecision of character, and the want of a
virtuous soul, have rendered him despicable [monstrous] in the eyes of the
good, and contemptible in the just opinion of the bad. In seeking to please
tyrants, he has lost the favor of all. And alas, the true church of Christ can no
longer pray for the success of his truckling [yielding] administration. It has
given their souls to the oppressor, and their bodies to the prison, if they dare
do their duty in obedience to Christ. In view of such facts, it is my candid
conviction that the record of the infernal regions [hell] can exhibit no blacker
deeds than the American archives, and the accursed Fugitive Slave Bill.
Upright humanity cannot uphold the hand that signed that bill of abomina-
tions [hateful things], unless it first does violence to its own nature. . . .

HRW material copyrighted under notice appearing earlier in this work.

I am proud to say that Patrick Henry's motto is mine—"Give me Liberty or give me Death." I am frank to declare that it is my fixed and changeless purpose to kill any so-called man who attempts to enslave me or mine, if possible, though it be Millard Fillmore himself. To do this, in defence of personal liberty, to my mind, would be an act of the highest virtue, and white Americans must be real hypocrites if they say not to it—amen!

Do they not *saint* the spirits of '76 for their noble defence of their inalienable [permanent] rights? Why then damn me for doing the same? 'Tis the joyful voice of a free people. . . . Who that is oppressed himself, is not ready to do the like deeds for his race to come? . . . I am ready, willing, and should rejoice to die; and I glory in the fact that so many of my brethren in tribulation [hardship] are of the same mind, and feel determined to be sacrificed rather than be enslaved. God grant that their number may be increased a thousand fold. . . .

And now, friends of the beloved Jesus, can you and will you stand quietly and see your Savior kidnapped in the person of his poor? Remember, if you suffer it to be done unto one of the least of his brethren [brothers], you suffer it to be done unto him.

Professors of religion, can you and will you permit, silently, the American Congress to pass a bill bidding all its citizens to aid in the enslaving of the Son of God? It is your duty to let the word "repeal! *repeal!!* REPEAL!!! go forth, backed up by the Christian's motto, "resistance to tyrants is obedience to God."

And you, my brethren, the objects of hate and the victims of oppression, can you and will you allow yourselves to be made the dupes [fools] of despots and the slaves of tyrants, without resisting even to death? I hope not. Disgrace not your nature. Be not recreant to [Do not abandon] your God. Allow not posterity [future generations] to curse thy memory and disown thy name for a base submission to avaricious [greedy] knaves.

That you may "show yourself a MAN," is the constant and ardent prayer of Your brother in bonds,


W. P. NEWMAN

--------------------------------------------------------------------------------

From the *North Star*, 24 October 1850, in *The Black Abolitionist Papers*, Volume IV, edited by C. Peter Ripley. Copyright © 1991 by The University of North Carolina Press.


**UNDERSTANDING WHAT YOU READ**   After you have finished reading the selection, answer the following questions in the space provided.

**1.** Who does William P. Newman compare President Fillmore and his followers to?

_____

_____

HRW material copyrighted under notice appearing earlier in this work.

**2.** What motto does Newman say is his own?

_____

_____

**3.** Why does Newman believe that white Americans are hypocrites?

_____

_____

**4.** What does he urge Christians to do? What does he encourage slaves to do?

_____

_____

## ACTIVITY

Imagine that you are a U.S. citizen who is writing to President Fillmore asking for a repeal of the Fugitive Slave Act. On a separate sheet of paper, write a letter stating your reasons for urging the repeal of the act. Try to include reasons beyond those listed by Newman.

HRW material copyrighted under notice appearing earlier in this work.

## LITERATURE READING

### *Narrative of the Life of Frederick Douglass, an American Slave*

*The story of the life of Frederick Douglass is a good example of the fugitive-slave narratives that were popular in the North before the Civil War. The account, written in 1845, details the story of Douglass's life from early childhood until his escape from bondage in 1838. He escaped by disguising himself as a sailor and fleeing to free territory. After gaining his freedom, Douglass worked passionately for the abolition of slavery as a powerful public speaker, editor of his own outspoken weekly newspaper, and close friend of radical abolitionist John Brown. After the Civil War, he continued to work for equal rights for all citizens, including women, and was committed to removing racial barriers and prejudices of every kind. As you read the excerpt, pay attention to Douglass's description of how slaves were valued.*

In a very short time after I went to live at Baltimore, my old master's youngest son Richard died; and in about three years and six months after his death, my old master, Captain Anthony died, leaving only his son, Andrew, and daughter, Lucretia, to share his estate. . . . Cut off thus unexpectedly, he left no will as to the disposal of his property. It was therefore necessary to have a valuation of the property, that it might be equally divided between Mrs. Lucretia and Master Andrew. I was immediately sent for, to be valued with the other property. Here again my feelings rose up in detestation [stong hatred] of slavery. Prior to this, I had become, if not insensible [accustomed] to my lot, at least partly so. I left Baltimore with a young heart overborne with sadness, and a soul full of apprehension [anxiety]. . . .

We were all ranked together at the valuation. Men and women, old and young, married and single, were ranked with horses, sheep, and swine. There were horses and men, cattle and women, pigs and children, all holding the same rank in the scale of being, and were all subjected to the same narrow examination. Silvery-headed age and sprightly youth, maids and matrons, had to undergo the same indelicate inspection. At this moment, I saw more clearly than ever the brutalizing effects of slavery upon both slave and slaveholder.

After the valuation, then came the division. I have no language to express the high excitement and deep anxiety which were felt among us poor slaves during this time. Our fate for life was now to be decided. We had no more voice in that decision than the brutes among whom we were ranked. A single word from the white men was enough—against all our wishes, prayers, and entreaties—to sunder [separate] forever the dearest friends, dearest kindred, and strongest ties known to human beings. . . .

HRW material copyrighted under notice appearing earlier in this work

I suffered more anxiety than most of my fellow slaves. I had known what it was to be kindly treated; they had known nothing of the kind. They had seen little or nothing of the world. They were in very deed men and women of sorrow, and acquainted with grief. Their back had been made familiar with the bloody lash, so that they had become callous [hardened]; mine was yet tender; for while at Baltimore I got few whippings, and few slaves could boast of a kinder master and mistress than myself; and the thought of passing out of their hands into those of Master Andrew—a man who, but a few days before, to give me a sample of his bloody disposition [personality], took my little brother by the throat, threw him on the ground, and with the heel of his boot stamped upon his head till the blood gushed from his nose and ears—was well calculated to make me anxious as to my fate. After he had committed this savage outrage [attack] upon my brother, he turned to me, and said that was the way he meant to serve me one of these days,—meaning, I suppose, when I came into his possession.

Thanks to a kind Providence [God], I fell to the portion of Mrs. Lucretia, and was sent immediately back to Baltimore, to live again in the family of Master Hugh. Their joy at my return equaled their sorrow at my departure. It was a glad day to me. I had escaped a fate worse than the lion's jaws.

--------------------------------------------------------------------

From *Narrative of the Life of Frederick Douglass, an American Slave* in *The Norton Anthology of American Literature:* Third Edition, Volume 1. Copyright © 1989 by W. W. Norton & Company, Inc.

**UNDERSTANDING WHAT YOU READ**   After you have finished reading the selection, answer the following questions in the space provided.

1. Why were slaves required to take part in the valuation process before the dividing of the estate?

_____

_____

2. What type of items were the slaves grouped with for inspection at the valuation?

_____

_____

3. Why were the slaves so anxious about the division of the estate?

_____

_____

4. How did Douglass escape "a fate worse than the lion's jaws"?

_____

_____

HRW material copyrighted under notice appearing earlier in this work.

**5.** How does this passage illustrate Douglass's observation that slavery has a brutalizing effect "upon both slave and slaveholder"?

_____

_____

## ACTIVITY

Imagine that you have been chosen to create a mural that celebrates the life, struggle, and accomplishments of Frederick Douglass. On a separate sheet of paper, list some of the items or visual images that you would include in the mural and tell why you think they are important. You may want to search the Internet through the HRW Go site for examples of murals.

 go.hrw.com
**SA1 Murals**

HRW material copyrighted under notice appearing earlier in this work.

## BIOGRAPHY READING

# John C. Calhoun

*As abolitionists worked to have slavery outlawed in new states and territories, southern states began to feel that their economic livelihood and way of life were being threatened. One of the leading southern politicians was a man from South Carolina named John C. Calhoun. Calhoun is best remembered for his strong defense of slavery as being vital to the economic and social stability of the South.*

John C. Calhoun was born in 1782. His family owned a prosperous farm and many slaves in South Carolina near the Savannah River. After his father died in 1796, Calhoun took over some of the duties of the farm. At the urging of an older brother, however, Calhoun returned to school, graduating from Yale in 1804. After studying law for several years, Calhoun opened a law office near his home in South Carolina.

In 1808 Calhoun was elected to the South Carolina legislature and in 1810 to the U.S. Congress. Calhoun was a member of the famed War Hawks, a group in favor of a war against Britain, and eventually was appointed chair of the foreign affairs committee. During his third congressional term, Calhoun accepted the position of secretary of war in President James Monroe's cabinet. He was elected vice president in 1824 and 1828.

During the late 1820s and early 1830s, Calhoun began to publicly speak in defense of the South. When Congress passed several tariffs that he thought would be damaging to the southern economy, Calhoun created the doctrine of nullification. This doctrine stated that a law was immediately null and void if the people of that state thought it unconstitutional. Calhoun also believed that states had the right to secede from the nation.

As abolitionists continued to call for the end of slavery, Calhoun became one of the main defenders of the slave system. He tried to protect slavery by praising slaveholding, gaining friends in western states and territories, and warning the North of the dangers of southern desperation. In 1836 Calhoun declared that the abolition of slavery would destroy the South.

Calhoun continued to defend slavery after President John Tyler appointed him secretary of state. He was re-elected to the U.S. Senate in 1845, where he opposed the admission of California to the Union as a free state. In his last address to the Senate, Calhoun predicted the abolition of slavery by the North, the anger between the whites of the North and South, the emancipation of slaves, and a union between free slaves and the North to keep the South relatively powerless. However, none of the elected officials listened to his warnings.

HRW material copyrighted under notice appearing earlier in this work.

After Calhoun retired from the Senate, he continued to remain involved in public affairs. During the last years of his life, he traveled around the South speaking to groups and conventions. He continued to advise southern lawmakers about the path the nation was heading down over the issue of slavery. Calhoun died in 1850 at the age of 68. It is rumored that his last words before he died were "The South, the poor South."

**UNDERSTANDING WHAT YOU READ**   After you have finished reading the selection, answer the following questions in the space provided.

**1.** What group was Calhoun associated with when he was first elected to Congress?

_____

_____

**2.** How did Calhoun try to protect the slavery system?

_____

_____

**3.** What was the doctrine of nullification that Calhoun created?

_____

_____

**4.** What did Calhoun predict in his final address to the Senate?

_____

_____

**ACTIVITY**

On a separate sheet of paper, write what you think would be a proper epitaph for John C. Calhoun.

HRW material copyrighted under notice appearing earlier in this work.

# PRIMARY SOURCE READING

## *A Confederate Girl's Diary*

*Many accounts of the Civil War have focused on battlefield conditions and the lives of soldiers. These rugged tales are balanced, however, by the warmer, more humane diaries and memoirs left by women from both sides. The wartime diary of Sarah Morgan Dawson was first published in 1913 and is one of the most popular of this particular type of writing. The diary chronicles the experiences of the Morgan family, who lived in Baton Rouge, Louisiana, and offers many insights into the lively personality and wit of Sarah Morgan herself. As you read the excerpt, consider the difficulties and dangers faced by civilians, particularly women, during the war.*

August 21st.

Miriam and mother are going to Baton Rouge in a few hours, to see if anything can be saved from the general wreck. From the reports of the removal of the Penitentiary machinery, State Library, Washington Statue, etc., we presume that that part of the town yet standing is to be burnt like the rest. I think, though, that mother has delayed too long. However, I dreamed last night that we had saved a great deal, in trunks; and my dreams sometimes come true. Waking with that impression, I was surprised, a few hours after, to hear mother's sudden determination. But I also dreamed I was about to marry a Federal officer! That was in consequence [as a result] of having answered the question, whether I would do so, with an emphatic "Yes! if I loved him," which will probably ruin my reputation as a patriot in this parish [Louisiana county]. Bah! I am no bigot!—or fool either. . . .

August 23rd.

Yesterday Anna and I spent the day with Lilly, and the rain in the evening obliged us to stay all night. Dr. Perkins stopped there, and repeated the same old stories we have been hearing, about the powder placed under the State House and Garrison, to blow them up, if forced to evacuate the town. He confirms the story about all the convicts being set free, and the town being pillaged [robbed] by the negroes and the rest of the Yankees. He says his own slaves told him they were allowed to enter the houses and help themselves, and what they did not want the Yankees either destroyed on the spot, or had it carried to the Garrison and burned. They also bragged of having stopped ladies on the street, cut their necklaces from their necks, and stripped the rings from their fingers, without hesitation. It may be that they were just bragging to look great in the eyes of their masters; I hope so, for Heaven help them if they fall into the hands of the Confederates, if it is true.

HRW material copyrighted under notice appearing earlier in this work.

I could not record all the stories of wanton destruction that reached us. I would rather not believe that the Federal Government could be so disgraced by its own soldiers. Dr. Day says they left nothing at all in his house, and carried everything off from Dr. Enders's. He does not believe we have a single article left in ours. . . .

This morning Withers's battery passed Mr. Elder's on their way to Port Hudson, and stopped to get water. There were several buckets served by several servants; but I took possession of one, to their great amusement. What a profusion [great quantity] of thanks over a can of water! It made me smile, and they smiled to see my work, so it was all very funny. It was astonishing to see the number of Yankee canteens in the possession of our men. Almost all those who fought at Baton Rouge are provided with them. . . . I declare I felt ever so important in my new situation as waiting-maid!

There is very little we would not do for our soldiers, though. There is mother, for instance, who got on her knees to bathe the face and hands of a fever-struck soldier of the Arkansas, while the girls held the plates of those who were too weak to hold them and eat at the same time. Blessed is the Confederate soldier who has even a toothache, when there are women near! What sympathies and remedies are volunteered!

-----------------------------------------------------------------------

From *A Confederate Girl's Diary* by Sarah Morgan Dawson. Copyright © 1960 by Indiana University Press.

**UNDERSTANDING WHAT YOU READ**   After you have finished reading the selection, answer the following questions in the space provided.

**1.** Why are Sarah Morgan's mother and Miriam going to Baton Rouge? Why is Morgan surprised?

_____

_____

**2.** What does Morgan say may ruin her reputation as a patriot?

_____

_____

**3.** What does Dr. Perkins say is happening in Baton Rouge?

_____

_____

**4.** How does Morgan help the Confederate soldiers? What is their response?

_____

_____

HRW material copyrighted under notice appearing earlier in this work.

**5.** Why do you think many women felt that it was important to talk to soldiers and to constantly gather news about the war?

_____

_____

### ACTIVITY

Imagine that you have been chosen to create a museum exhibit about the Civil War. On a separate sheet of paper, create a plan for what information you would like to convey and what artifacts you would exhibit as part of the display. Be sure to include in your plan some information about military and civilian life in the North and the South. You may want to search the Internet through the HRW Go site for samples of exhibits.

 go.hrw.com
**SA1 Museum**

HRW material copyrighted under notice appearing earlier in this work.

## LITERATURE READING

### *Miss Ravenel's Conversion from Secession to Loyalty*

*After the Civil War, many authors wrote about the suffering and death they had seen. John William De Forest, who served as a captain in the Union army, published his novel* Miss Ravenel's Conversion from Secession to Loyalty *in 1867. This novel was one of the first American works of literary realism, a style of fictional writing that truthfully depicts common, everyday life. Literary realism became popular in the late 1800s. The following passage describes the wounding of Captain Colburne, the main character in the novel. As you read the excerpt, pay attention to the ways De Forest uses details to make his story more realistic.*

When Colburne came to himself he was lying on the ground. . . . Beside him . . . lay a wounded lieutenant . . . and four wounded artillerists. A dozen steps away, rapidly blackening in the scorching sun and sweltering [very humid] air, were two more artillerists, stark dead, one with his brains bulging from a bullet-hole in his forehead while a dark claret-colored [burgundy-colored] streak crossed his face, the other's light-blue trousers soaked with a dirty carnation [red] stain of life-blood. . . .

Deep in the . . . woods, a full mile and a half from the fighting line, [Colburne and some of his men] came to the field hospital of the division. It was simply an immense collection of wounded men in every imaginable condition of mutilation [physical injury], every one stained more or less with his own blood, every one of a ghastly yellowish pallor [paleness], all lying in the open air on the bare ground or on their own blankets with no shelter except the friendly foliage [leaves] of the oaks and beeches. . . .

Colburne refused one or two offers to dress his wound, saying that others needed more instant care than himself. When at last he submitted to an examination, it was found that the ball had passed between the bones of the fore-arm, not breaking them indeed, but scaling off some exterior splinters and making an ugly rent [tear] in the muscles. . . .

His arm was swollen to twice its natural size from the knuckles to the elbow. . . . During the night previous to this journey . . . he could only escape from his painful self-consciousness by drenching himself with chloroform [anaesthetic]. . . .

In St. Stephen's Hospital Colburne found something of that comfort which a wounded man needs. His arm was dressed for the second time; his ragged uniform, stiff with blood and dirt, was removed; he was sponged from head to foot and laid in the first sheets he had seen for months. There were three other wounded officers in the room. . . . A major of a Connecticut

HRW material copyrighted under notice appearing earlier in this work.

regiment, who had received a grapeshot [gunshot] through the lungs, smiled at Colburne's arm and whispered, "Flea bite." Then he pointed to the horrible orifice [hole] in his own breast, through which the blood and breath could be seen to bubble whenever the dressings were removed.

---

From *Miss Ravenel's Conversion from Secession to Loyalty* by John William De Forest, 1867.

**UNDERSTANDING WHAT YOU READ**   After you have finished reading the selection, answer the following questions in the space provided.

**1.** How far did Captain Colburne and his men have to travel to a field hospital? What was the hospital like?

_____

_____

**2.** Why does Captain Colburne refuse to have his wound dressed?

_____

_____

**3.** How does Captain Colburne deal with the pain from the infection in his arm?

_____

_____

**4.** Based on the passage, how effective do you think medical care was during the Civil War?

_____

_____

**5.** Provide an example from the text that shows it is a work of literary realism.

_____

_____

**ACTIVITY**

Imagine that you are a soldier who has been wounded during the Civil War. On a separate sheet of paper, write a letter to your family describing what happened after you were wounded, the kind of treatment you received, and what events occurred around you.

HRW material copyrighted under notice appearing earlier in this work.

**CHAPTER 19**

**The Civil War**

★ ★ ★ ★ ★ ★ ★ ★ ★ ★ ★ ★ ★ ★ ★ ★ ★ ★ ★ ★ ★ ★ ★ ★

# BIOGRAPHY READING

## Clara Barton

*Clara Barton is most famous for founding the American Red Cross. Before she founded the organization, Barton helped wounded soldiers during the Civil War. She was also a great supporter of women's suffrage and equal pay for equal work. Clara Barton is probably best remembered for her heroism on the battlefield and for providing relief to soldiers and disaster victims when most needed.*

Clara Barton was born on December 25, 1821, in Oxford, Massachusetts. Her parents and older siblings taught her literature, math, and outdoor sports. Although she was very shy, Barton became a teacher.

In 1850 Barton enrolled at the Liberal Institute of Clinton, New York. She then went on to establish one of the first public schools in New Jersey. The school became so successful that the trustees no longer wanted a woman to run it. Barton, however, refused to work for a male principal. From 1854 to 1861 Barton worked for the U.S. Patent Office, where she encountered more discrimination in the form of hostility from her male co-workers.

When the Civil War broke out in 1861, Barton used her organizational skills to collect food and medical supplies for the men wounded at the Battle of Bull Run. She was concerned about the lack of supplies and basic first aid, and was granted permission to travel through battle lines to search for missing soldiers, nurse wounded men, and bring badly needed supplies. Her heroic efforts and great personal sacrifices during the Civil War earned her the nickname Angel of the Battlefield.

In 1869 Barton provided relief work during the Franco-Prussian War. While in Europe she learned of the formation of the International Red Cross and its activities. She returned to the United States in 1877, and in 1881 organized the American Red Cross. The American Red Cross provides aid during times of war, droughts, floods, outbreaks of disease, railway accidents, and other domestic disasters. Under Barton's leadership, the organization responded to many disasters, such as the Johnstown flood in Pennsylvania, a forest fire in Michigan, an outbreak of yellow fever in Florida, and a hurricane in Galveston, Texas, in 1900.

During Barton's term as the head of the American Red Cross, some of her management practices came under criticism. She was finally forced to resign in 1904 when the federal government threatened to cut off funds to the organization. After her resignation, however, Barton remained active and connected to the cause. She was planning to establish a Red Cross organization in Mexico at the time of her death in 1912, at the age of 91.

HRW material copyrighted under notice appearing earlier in this work

**UNDERSTANDING WHAT YOU READ**   After you have finished reading the
selection, answer the following questions in the space provided.

**1.** What types of opposition did Clara Barton encounter during her life?

_____

_____

**2.** What did Barton do during the Civil War? What was her nickname?

_____

_____

**3.** What did Barton do after she returned from working with the International Red Cross?

_____

_____

**4.** Under what circumstances does the American Red Cross provide aid?

_____

_____

**ACTIVITY**

Imagine that you are a reporter who is going to interview Clara Barton. On
a separate sheet of paper, come up with a list of 10 questions you would ask.
Then find a partner in your class, and take turns playing the roles of the
interviewer and Barton. Write down the answers to your questions.

HRW material copyrighted under notice appearing earlier in this work.

## Reconstruction

★ ★ ★ ★ ★ ★ ★ ★ ★ ★ ★ ★ ★ ★ ★ ★ ★ ★ ★ ★ ★ ★ ★ ★ ★ ★ ★

# PRIMARY SOURCE READING

## *Plessy v. Ferguson*

*In 1890 Louisiana passed a law requiring "separate but equal" passenger cars for black and white railroad travelers. In 1892 Homer Plessy, an African American man, was arrested for attempting to ride in a car reserved for white travelers. When lower courts upheld the law, Plessy appealed his case—called Plessy v. Ferguson—to the Supreme Court. In 1896 the Court ruled 7-1 against him. Justice Henry Brown wrote for the majority in the case. For almost 60 years states used this decision to continue a system of legal segregation. As you read the excerpt, consider how Justice Brown views the purpose of legislation as well as the content of a specific law.*

The constitutionality of this act is attacked upon the ground that it conflicts both with the Thirteenth Amendment of the Constitution, abolishing slavery, and the Fourteenth Amendment, which prohibits certain restrictive legislation on the part of the States. . . .

A statute [law] which implies merely a legal distinction between the white and colored races . . . founded in the color of the two races . . . has no tendency to destroy the legal equality of the two races, or re-establish a state of involuntary servitude [slavery]. . . . [T]he Thirteenth Amendment is . . . relied upon by the plaintiff [Homer Plessy] in error in this connection. . . .

The object of the [Fourteenth Amendment] was undoubtedly to enforce the absolute equality of the two races before the law, but . . . it could not have been intended to abolish distinctions based upon color, or to enforce social, as distinguished from political, equality, or a commingling of the two races upon terms unsatisfactory to either. Laws permitting, and even requiring, their separation . . . do not necessarily imply the inferiority of either race to the other. . . .

We consider the underlying fallacy [weakness] of the plaintiff's argument to consist in the assumption that the enforced separation of the two races stamps the colored race with a badge of inferiority. If this be so, it is not by reason of anything found in the act. . . . The argument also assumes that social prejudices may be overcome by legislation, and that equal rights cannot be secured to the negro except by an enforced commingling [interaction] of the two races. We cannot accept this proposition.

HRW material copyrighted under notice appearing earlier in this work.

**UNDERSTANDING WHAT YOU READ**   After you have finished reading the selection, answer the following questions in the space provided.

1. What parts of the U.S. Constitution did Homer Plessy believe the separate passenger cars law violated?

_____

_____

2. What does Justice Brown say about a law that implies "merely a legal distinction between the white and colored races"?

_____

_____

3. What does Justice Brown say is the object of the Fourteenth Amendment? What does he say is not its purpose?

_____

_____

4. What does the majority opinion say is the underlying weakness of Plessy's argument?

_____

_____

5. How long was the majority decision in *Plessy* v. *Ferguson* used by states to uphold segregation laws?

_____

_____

## ACTIVITY

Imagine that you are an illustrator for a northern newspaper in the 1890s and that you have been asked to draw a picture to accompany an article about Homer Plessy's arrest. Create a sketch of the scene on the railroad car and write a caption that points out how "separate but equal" treatment was unfair.

HRW material copyrighted under notice appearing earlier in this work.

## CHAPTER 20 — Reconstruction

★ ★ ★ ★ ★ ★ ★ ★ ★ ★ ★ ★ ★ ★ ★ ★ ★ ★ ★ ★ ★ ★ ★

# LITERATURE READING

## "Jim Crow Cars"

*The Jim Crow laws of the Reconstruction era legalized segregation in transportation, schools, parks, and other public places. African American poet Lizelia Augusta Jenkins Moorer protested against the humiliation caused by such legalized discrimination. Although her poems speak with strong emotion, Moorer supports her arguments with concrete examples. As you read the poem, which was published in 1907, consider the problems faced by African Americans under segregation.*

### JIM CROW CARS

If within the cruel Southland you have chanced to take a ride,
You the Jim Crow cars have noticed, how they crush a Negro's pride,
How he pays a first class passage and a second class receives,
Gets the worst accommodations ev'ry friend of truth believes.

'Tis the rule that all conductors, in the service of the train,
Practice gross[1] discriminations on the Negro—such is plain—
If a drunkard is a white man, at his mercy Negroes are,
Legalized humiliation is the Negro Jim Crow car.

'Tis a license given white men, they may go just where they please,
In the white man's car or Negro's will they move with perfect ease,
If complaint is made by Negroes the conductor will go out
Till the whites are through carousing, then he shows himself about.

They will often raise a riot, butcher up the Negroes there,
Unmolested will they quarrel, use their pistols, rant[2] and swear,
They will smoke among the ladies though offensive the cigar;
'Tis the place to drink their whiskey, in the Negro Jim Crow car.

If a Negro shows resistance to his treatment by a tough,
At some station he's arrested for the same, though not enough,
He is thrashed or lynched or tortured as will please the demon's rage,
Mobbed, of course, by "unknown parties," thus is closed the darkened page.

----

From Lizelia Augusta Jenkins Moorer. In *Collected Black Women's Poetry*.
Oxford University Press, 1988.

----

[1] extreme
[2] talk loudly

HRW material copyrighted under notice appearing earlier in this work.

**UNDERSTANDING WHAT YOU READ**   After you have finished reading the selection, answer the following questions in the space provided.

**1.** What are the "Jim Crow cars" that the author refers to?

_____

_____

**2.** What does the author mean when she says that Jim Crow cars are "legalized humiliation"? What are some examples of the humiliation suffered by African Americans who rode in those cars?

_____

_____

**3.** According to the author, what happened if an African American passenger complained to the conductor about the behavior of white men in the car?

_____

_____

**4.** According to the author, what happened to an African American passenger who resisted abuse by a white man?

_____

_____

**5.** How do you think the author feels about the concept of "separate but equal"? Who does the author think benefits most by legal segregation?

_____

_____

## ACTIVITY

Imagine that you are an African American who has just had to travel by train in the South during Reconstruction. Write an editorial to your local newspaper describing the troubles you experienced and what should be done to change the situation.

HRW material copyrighted under notice appearing earlier in this work.

★ ★ ★ ★ ★ ★ ★ ★ ★ ★ ★ ★ ★ ★ ★ ★ ★ ★ ★ ★ ★ ★ ★

# BIOGRAPHY READING

## George Washington Carver

*George Washington Carver was a distinguished African American teacher and scientist. He developed more than 300 uses for the peanut and some 118 for the sweet potato. His agricultural research benefited many southern farmers, who were too dependent on growing cotton.*

George Washington Carver was born near Diamond Grove, Missouri, to slave parents. The exact date of his birth is unknown, but it was probably sometime in 1864. His father died shortly after Carver was born. While still an infant, Carver and his mother were kidnapped by slave raiders from Arkansas. He was soon brought back to Diamond Grove by a neighbor, but he never saw or heard from his mother again.

Carver was taken in by Moses and Susan Carver, his mother's former owners. The Carvers gave him their last name and raised him like their own son. From an early age, George Carver displayed a sharp intellect and a deep interest in nature. However, African Americans were not allowed to attend the local grammar school. Thus, when he was about 12 years old, he left Diamond Grove in search of a formal education.

Carver spent the next several years moving around the Midwest, where he attended various grade schools and worked at odd jobs to support himself. He went to high school during the early 1880s in Minneapolis, Kansas. In 1885 he was again refused admission to a school—this time a small college in Kansas— because of his race. After five more years working as a farmer, hotel cook, and laundryman, Carver was finally admitted to Simpson College in Indianola, Iowa, in 1890.

Carver studied piano and art while he was at Simpson College, but in 1891 he decided to study agriculture full time. He transferred to Iowa State Agricultural College, where he received a bachelor's degree in agricultural science in 1894 and a master of science degree in 1896. While a student at Iowa State, Carver gained a reputation as an extremely gifted student of botany, or plant science.

In 1896 Carver accepted a job as director of a new agricultural department at the Tuskegee Institute, a college and vocational school for African Americans in Alabama. He had been hired by Booker T. Washington, a well-known African American educator. Carver would remain on the Tuskegee faculty for the rest of his life.

Carver's schedule at Tuskegee was a busy one. Along with teaching classes, conducting research, and supervising an experimental farm, he published bulletins offering advice to farmers. He also established a "movable school of agriculture" that provided equipment, field demonstrations, and home economics classes to poor farmers in Alabama.

HRW material copyrighted under notice appearing earlier in this work.

Carver's most famous work, however, dealt with peanuts. He believed that southern farmers devoted too much land to raising cotton, a cash crop that depleted the soil of nutrients. He urged them to grow a variety of staple crops instead. Peanuts were an especially good crop to grow, Carver explained, because they were high in protein and restored nitrogen (a nutrient necessary for plants) to the soil. In an effort to make peanuts more profitable for farmers, Carver set up a laboratory devoted to finding new uses for them. Throughout his career, he developed more than 300 peanut-based products, including new types of flour, ink, dye, plastic, soap, cosmetics, and medicine.

In 1940 Carver used his life savings to establish the George Washington Carver Foundation, a fund for agricultural research at Tuskegee. He died of anemia in early 1943. Later that year, his birthplace was made a national monument by Congress.

**UNDERSTANDING WHAT YOU READ**   After you have finished reading the selection, answer the following questions in the space provided.

**1.** How did Carver obtain his early education?

_____

_____

**2.** What subject did Carver study at Simpson College? Why did he transfer to Iowa State?

_____

_____

**3.** What were five of Carver's activities at the Tuskegee Institute?

_____

_____

**4.** Why did Carver think southern farmers should grow peanuts?

_____

_____

**5.** What was the George Washington Carver Foundation?

_____

_____

## ACTIVITY

Imagine that you are a fellow of Britain's Royal Society for the Arts. On a separate sheet of paper, write a short paragraph nominating Carver for membership.

HRW material copyrighted under notice appearing earlier in this work.

Name _____ Class _____ Date _____

## PRIMARY SOURCE READING

# Cowhands and Cattle Drives

*Cowboys driving longhorns across the Great Plains to cattle towns during the mid-1800s encountered many adventures. Cattle drives were physically demanding, and working cattle trails could be dangerous, with threats from rustlers, or cattle thieves, and stampedes. The following excerpts describe life in the Cattle Kingdom. As you read the selection, pay attention to the challenges faced by cowboys during cattle drives.*

I wasn't nineteen years old when I come up the trail. . . . The average age of cowboys then . . . was twenty-three or four. Except for the bosses there was very few thirty-year-old men on the trail.

Look at the chances they took and the kind of riding they done . . . over rough country. Even in the daytime those deep coulees [gullies] could open up all at once, . . . before you had a chance to see where you were going, and at night it was something awful if you'd stop to think about it, which none of them ever did. If a storm come and the cattle started running—you'd hear that low rumbling noise along the ground and the men on the herd wouldn't need to come in and tell you, you'd know—then you'd jump for your horse and get out there in the lead, trying to head them and get them into a mill [circular motion] before they scattered. . . . It was riding at a dead run in the dark, with cut banks [sharp drop-offs] and prairie dog holes all around you, not knowing if the next jump would land you in a shallow grave.

We were camped close to Blue River. . . . That night it come up an awful storm. It took all four of us to hold the cattle and we didn't hold them, and when morning come there was one man missing. We went back to look for him, and we found him among the prairie dog holes, beside his horse. The horse's ribs was scraped bare of hide, and all the rest of horse and man was mashed into the ground as flat as a pancake. The only thing you could recognize was the handle of his six-shooter. We tried to think the lightning hit him, and that was what we wrote his folks down in Henrietta, Texas. But we couldn't really believe it ourselves. . . . I'm afraid his horse stepped into one of them holes and they both went down before the stampede.

But the awful part of it was that we had milled them cattle over him all night, not knowing he was there. That was what we couldn't get out of our minds. And after that, orders were given to sing when you were running with a stampede, so the others would know where you were. . . . After awhile this grew to be a custom on the range.

[Rustlers] would follow you up for days with a pack horse, waiting [for] their chance and keeping out of sight. . . . A dark night was what they were looking for, especially if it was raining hard, because the rain would wash out

HRW material copyrighted under notice appearing earlier in this work.

the tracks. . . . They would watch you as you rode around the herd on night guard . . . then . . . they would slip up to the other side of the herd and pop [wave] a blanket. And the whole herd would get up like one animal and light out [all begin running at once]. These rustlers had very good horses, and they would cut in ahead of you as you tried to get up in front of the herd, and would cut off anywhere from fifty to two hundred head of . . . steers.

–E. C. Abbott "Teddy Blue"

From "Up the Trail in '79" from *We Pointed Them North: Recollections of a Cowpuncher* by E. C. Abbott and Helena Huntington Smith. Copyright 1939 by Farrar & Rinehart, Inc.; copyright 1954 by the **University of Oklahoma Press.** Reprinted by permission of the publisher.

[the Red River] looked to be a mile wide, but it was not swimming deep except for a short distance. . . . When I reached the river the cattle were going in nicely, and the only trouble we had was when some of the cattle bogged [got stuck] and we had to pull them out. . . . A day or two after this Richter and Kees [two cowhands] had a fight [about how to drive the cattle] in which Kees was shot.

[We] were going across a very dry country . . . and the herd had no water for two days. There was just a small breeze from the west, but the cattle smelled water and as I looked ahead I could see the men working diligently [hard] and fast with the lead cattle [to keep them from stampeding toward the water], but with little success. The men from further down the line ran as fast as they could to help, but about a thousand head of big long-horn cattle had smelled the water that the breeze had wafted [carried] toward them. They were bawling, switching their tails and clashing their horns together and were gradually gaining ground on the men.

–James C. Shaw

**UNDERSTANDING WHAT YOU READ**   After you have finished reading the selection, answer the following questions in the space provided.

**1.** According to the first passage, what was the average age of cowhands on the trail?

_____

_____

**2.** What were some of the dangers that cowhands faced on cattle drives?

_____

_____

HRW material copyrighted under notice appearing earlier in this work.

**3.** Why did cowhands begin the custom of singing when they were running with a stampede?

_____

_____

**4.** How would cattle rustlers go about stealing a herd from the cowhands?

_____

_____

**5.** What do you think would be the most difficult part of being a cowhand? What would be the most rewarding part?

_____

_____

## ACTIVITY

Imagine that you are producing a movie about the life of a cowboy. Create a movie poster that features a cattle drive. Be sure to include a title for your movie, as well as an attention-getting phrase that accurately describes the movie's plot, characters, or message.

HRW material copyrighted under notice appearing earlier in this work.

## LITERATURE READING

# *The Life of an Ordinary Woman*

*Most accounts of frontier mining society were written by men and focused on subjects like the location of mines. The Life of an Ordinary Woman by Anne Ellis is a first-person account that includes information about children and women living in western mining towns. The book also illustrates the economic challenges miners faced. As you read the selection, note Ellis's descriptions of her mother's activities.*

I do not know how far it is from Christian County, Missouri, to Custer County, Colorado, but it must have seemed far, traveling with oxen. I can almost hear my father say, "These old mossbacked backwoods Missourians are dead in the shell and don't know it. We will go West where there are chances for a man, and there we will found our fortunes."

And such chances as there were, too! Think of the farming land they passed, and of the fine ranches they drove over! Only they were not looking for ranches—they wanted mines, where, as they thought, riches came overnight and without work.

Did my young mother dread this journey, or look forward to it? I think that, in spite of the fear of the Indians (and this was a dreadful fear), she did look forward with her heart full of hope. . . .

My father was the kind who traveled, trusting Fate to provide, and it did—but Mama was fate! . . . She would look forward and be happy, thinking of the home she was going to have "out there," and then look back and cry, thinking of the friends she had left. She was like this. I would have only looked forward. With all the work and hardships, she was "eating her white bread" then, although she did not know it. At night my father would bring out his banjo—all day he would have a headache and would have to lie in the wagon. It was cured when the sun went down and the day's work was over. Then they would all sit around the camp-fire, and sing, and some would dance. . . . All troubles were forgotten while they planned the things they would have, and do, when they "struck it rich." . . .

Always, when I think of pioneers, I see my mother, a baby on her arm, working, working, ever hopeful, seeing something to laugh at, cooking for the men, feeding the cattle at night, doctoring both the men and cattle. She was a born doctor. In after years she would go any time of the day or night to bring some one's baby into the world, doing everything and then finishing up with the washing. They might say, "You know you are not a regular doctor so cannot charge anything, but we will give you five or ten dollars." Sometimes they did and sometimes they did not. But it was all the same to her if they needed help.

HRW material copyrighted under notice appearing earlier in this work.

We did not stay very long in any place, and were always poverty-stricken. We came into Pueblo and camped at the edge of town, with nothing to eat. And this brave country woman leaving her baby in camp with oh! such a fear pulling at her heart that the baby might toddle out under the feet of the oxen or fall into the fire, or into the evil-looking Arkansas river, took one of her most prized possessions, a pieced quilt, and went into the city to sell it for food. While she would not be afraid when the mad buffalo charged down on them, the noise, the unfriendliness of the rushing crowds in this strange city, did raise such a lump in her throat, such a weakness in her stomach, but she went bravely on. In after years, she felt it a disgrace that she had once begged in Pueblo. Thus it is, some of the noblest things we do we are ashamed of, and sometimes are proud of such little, piffly things.

-------------------------------------------------------------

From Chapter II (retitled "Westward Movement") from *The Life of an Ordinary Woman* by Anne Ellis. Copyright 1929 by Anne Ellis; copyright renewed © 1957 by Neita Carey and Earl E. Ellis. Reprinted by permission of *Houghton Mifflin Company.*

## UNDERSTANDING WHAT YOU READ   After you have finished reading the selection, answer the following questions in the space provided.

**1.** Why, according to Ellis, did her father want to be a miner?

_____

_____

**2.** What kind of opportunities did Ellis's parents pass up as they traveled west?

_____

_____

**3.** What kinds of work did Ellis see her mother do during the journey?

_____

_____

**4.** How does Ellis tell the reader that her mother had pride?

_____

_____

## ACTIVITY

Imagine that you are a mine owner who needs to recruit workers. Write a want ad to be placed in various newspapers describing the kind of opportunities that mine workers would have, and how working for your company would be better than working for another mining operation.

HRW material copyrighted under notice appearing earlier in this work.

**CHAPTER**

**21**

## The West

★ ★ ★ ★ ★ ★ ★ ★ ★ ★ ★ ★ ★ ★ ★ ★ ★ ★ ★ ★ ★ ★

# BIOGRAPHY READING

## Sarah Winnemucca

*As settlers moved west, they sometimes came into conflict with the local American Indian tribes. These Indians were often moved off of their tradition-al homelands and onto reservations to make room for the farmers and ranch-ers settling the area. Outraged at the treatment of her people at the hands of the U.S. government, a Paiute Indian named Sarah Winnemucca began a campaign to improve the lives of American Indians.*

Sarah Winnemucca was a Paiute Indian who was born near Humboldt Lake, Nevada, around 1844. Both her father and grandfather were chiefs of the tribe, making Winnemucca a princess. In 1850 her grandfather took some of his family, including Winnemucca, to work on a ranch in the San Joaquin Valley in California. Winnemucca soon learned to speak Spanish and English.

At the dying request of her grandfather, Winnemucca was sent to school at St. Mary's Convent in San Jose, California. She had to leave school three weeks after she arrived because many white parents did not want her to be in class with their children. When she returned home, she found that her tribe had been moved to a reservation. Winnemucca began to see firsthand the problems associated with Indian agents who did little to help her people. The entire Paiute tribe was eventually forced to move to Oregon.

After the move, Winnemucca became the interpreter for Samuel Parrish, the only Indian agent she ever trusted. The Paiute had more bad luck when Samuel Parrish was transferred and Major William V. Rinehart was put in charge. He banished Winnemucca from the agency after she reported his bad conduct.

Beginning in 1870, Winnemucca—who now spoke Spanish, English, and three Indian languages fluently—began to give speeches about the plight of her people and to ask for assistance. To turn public opinion against her, her opponents began to spread destructive rumors about her credibility and character.

In 1880 Winnemucca traveled to Washington, D.C., to plead her people's cause before Secretary of the Interior Carl Scars and President Rutherford B. Hayes. Although Secretary Scars made many promises, he did not follow through with his pledges. About this time Winnemucca went to Vancouver, Washington, to teach school. Around 1882 Winnemucca again traveled to the East in order to gain support for actions that would help the Paiute. She gained many well-known supporters and gave lectures in New York, Rhode Island, Connecticut, Pennsylvania, Maryland, and Massachusetts. She even wrote a book, *Life Among the Piutes*, to make money to cover her travel expenses.

HRW material copyrighted under notice appearing earlier in this work.

In 1886 Winnemucca retired from teaching and lecturing and moved to live with her sister in Montana. She died of tuberculosis in 1891. Although she did not see a great deal of success from her efforts during her lifetime, she helped to inspire others to continue the struggle.

## UNDERSTANDING WHAT YOU READ
After you have finished reading the selection, answer the following questions in the space provided.

**1.** What American Indian tribe did Winnemucca belong to? Where did they live?

_____

_____

**2.** Why was Winnemucca sent away from St. Mary's Convent? What did she find upon her return home?

_____

_____

**3.** How did Winnemucca try to help her people?

_____

_____

**4.** Do you think Winnemucca's efforts were important even though they did not bring immediate changes? Explain your answer.

_____

_____

## ACTIVITY

Imagine that you have just heard a speech given by Sarah Winnemucca. On a separate sheet of paper, write a letter to your representative urging action to help the Paiute.

HRW material copyrighted under notice appearing earlier in this work.

## Modern America

★ ★ ★ ★ ★ ★ ★ ★ ★ ★ ★ ★ ★ ★ ★ ★ ★ ★ ★

# PRIMARY SOURCE READING

# The Path to the Atomic Bomb

*In 1946 Leo Szilard, a professor at the University of Chicago, delivered a public lecture on the history of atomic research leading up to the detonation of nuclear weapons. Szilard had been a key player in the development of nuclear power during his life. Born in Budapest, Hungary, he emigrated to the United States in 1938 to escape the growing influence of Adolf Hitler. In 1939 Szilard persuaded Albert Einstein to write a letter to U.S. president Franklin Roosevelt urging government support for research into military uses for atomic power. Szilard later joined the Manhattan Project and participated in the development of the first nuclear weapons. The selection below is excerpted from Szilard's lecture. As you read the selection, consider Szilard's attitude toward the use of nuclear weapons.*

As you probably know, it all started one day around the turn of the century when Becquerel in Paris noticed that uranium minerals, placed in a drawer near some photographic plates, blackened those plates. . . .

Madame Curie was at that point a graduate student with Becquerel, and she had a suspicion that uranium minerals contained some element other than uranium which was more active than uranium.

And as you know, years later she isolated radium from such minerals. . . .

Transmuting one chemical element into another chemical element was, as you know, the unsolved problem of the alchemists.

But Madame Curie, who isolated radium, could not pride herself to be a successful alchemist.

She did not produce radium.

She merely separated it chemically from a mineral in which it was previously contained. . . .

So, in spite of this new discovery, God remained the first and only successful alchemist.

Now, the discovery of artificial radioactivity had been predicted as early as 1914.

It had been predicted not by any physicist, but by H. G. Wells. Wells put this discovery into the year of 1933, the year in which it actually happened.

His book, called *The World Set Free,* was published before the First World War, and goes far beyond predicting Joliot's discovery.

It also predicts the large-scale liberation and industrial use of atomic energy, the manufacture of atomic bombs, and a world war in 1956 in which Chicago, Paris, London, and other cities are destroyed at the very outbreak of the war.

According to Wells, these cities are transformed into rubble, or to be quite precise, into radioactive rubble. . . .

HRW material copyrighted under notice appearing earlier in this work.

Apparently between the years of 1935 and 1938 I went through the process of becoming an expert, that is, a man who knows what cannot be done.

I have no apology to offer and my only consolation is that I was in very good company.

For fission really ought to have been discovered as early as 1934. . . .

The Swedish Academy has always been very anxious to avoid awarding the Nobel Prize for advances which might later turn out to have been in error and therefore in general it does not like to award the Nobel Prize for results which are derived by means of theory rather than by means of experiments. . . .

But unfortunately, truth in science is a rather elusive creature, and the principle of "safety first" is not a reliable guide for action in any field of human endeavor. . . .

It seems to me we ought to thank God that the fission of uranium was not discovered, as it should have been, in 1934 or 1935.

It is almost certain that if this discovery had been made at that time, with Germany planning for war and England and America being in the frame of mind in which they were, the Germans would have found a way to make a chain reaction and would have won the war within a few weeks after they started it.

Perhaps those of us who missed this discovery 12 years ago, ought to be considered as candidates for the next award of the Nobel Prize for Peace. . . .

With the production of plutonium carried out on an industrial scale during the war, the dream of the alchemists came true and now we can change, at will, one element into another.

That is more than [Madame] Curie could do.

But while the first successful alchemist was undoubtably God, I sometimes wonder whether the second successful alchemist may not have been the Devil himself.

--------------------------------------------------------------------------------

From "Creative Intelligence and Society: The Case of Atomic Research, The Background in Fundamental Science," from *The Collective Works of Leo Szilard: The Scientific Papers*, Volume I, edited by Bernard T. Feld and Gertrud Weiss Szilard. Copyright © 1972 by The Massachusetts Institute of Technology.

**UNDERSTANDING WHAT YOU READ**  After you have finished reading the selection, answer the following questions in the space provided.

**1.** Why does Szilard state that Madame Curie was not an alchemist even though she discovered radium? Who does Szilard say was the first and only successful alchemist?

_____

_____

**2.** Who does Szilard say predicted the discovery of artificial radioactivity? When was its discovery predicted to occur?

_____

_____

HRW material copyrighted under notice appearing earlier in this work.

**3.** Why does Szilard believe that he and his fellow scientists should be considered for the Noble Peace Prize for their failure to discover nuclear fission in the 1930s?

_____

_____

**4.** How does Szilard believe that an earlier discovery of nuclear fission would have affected World War II?

_____

_____

**5.** What does Szilard's reference to the Devil as the second successful alchemist reveal about his attitude toward the development of nuclear weapons?

_____

_____

## ACTIVITY

Imagine that you are a science fiction author like H. G. Wells. On a separate sheet of paper, predict a discovery or an invention that you think will occur within the next 30 years, and discuss how it could bring both benefits and dangers to the world.

HRW material copyrighted under notice appearing earlier in this work.

★ ★ ★ ★ ★ ★ ★ ★ ★ ★ ★ ★ ★ ★ ★ ★ ★ ★ ★ ★ ★ ★ ★ ★ ★ ★

# LITERATURE READING

## *The Autobiography of Malcolm X*

*Malcolm Little was was born on May 19, 1925, in Omaha, Nebraska. His father was a Baptist minister and a supporter of Marcus Garvey and the UNIA (United Negro Improvement Association). In 1946 Malcolm Little was imprisoned for robbery, and it was in prison that he began to read about and study the condition of African Americans. It was also in prison that Malcolm Little converted to the Black Muslim faith and changed his name to Malcolm X. After leaving prison, he became a widely known minister in the Nation of Islam. He preached black separatism, black nationalism, and pride in race and racial achievements. The following excerpt is from his 1965 autobiography. As you read the selection, think about the state of race relations today.*

They called me "the angriest Negro in America." I wouldn't deny that charge. I spoke exactly as I felt. "I *believe* in anger. The Bible says that there is a *time* for anger." They called me "a teacher, a fomenter [inciter] of violence." I would say point blank, "That is a lie. I'm not for wanton [unjustified] violence, I'm for justice. I feel that if white people were attacked by Negroes—if the forces of law prove unable, or inadequate, or reluctant to protect those whites from those Negroes—then those white people should protect and defend themselves from those Negroes, using arms if necessary. And I feel that when the law fails to protect Negroes from whites' attack, then those Negroes should use arms, if necessary, to defend themselves.". . .

"I *am* for violence if non-violence means we continue postponing a solution to the American black man's problems—just to *avoid* violence. I don't go for non-violence if it also means a delayed solution. To me a delayed solution is a non-solution. Or I'll say it another way. If it must take violence to get the black man his human rights in this country, I'm *for* . . . violence.". . .

I am in agreement one hundred per cent with those racists who say that no government laws can ever *force* brotherhood. The only true world solution today is governments guided by true religion—of the spirit. Here in race-torn America, I am convinced that the Islam religion is desperately needed, particularly by the American black man. . . .

"Since I learned the *truth* in Mecca, my dearest friends have come to include *all* kinds—some Christians, Jews, Buddhists, Hindus, agnostics, and even atheists! I have friends who are called capitalists, Socialists, and Communists! Some of my friends are moderates, conservatives,

HRW material copyrighted under notice appearing earlier in this work.

extremists—some are even Uncle Toms! My friends today are black, brown, red, yellow and *white*!". . .

I tell sincere white people, "Work in conjunction with us—each of us working among our own kind." Let sincere white individuals find all other white people they can who feel as they do—and let them form their own all-white groups, to work trying to convert other white people who are thinking and acting so racist. Let sincere whites go and teach non-violence to white people!

From *The Autobiography of Malcolm X* by Malcolm X with Alex Haley. Copyright © 1964 by Alex Haley and Malcolm X; copyright © 1965 by Alex Haley and Betty Shabazz. Reprinted by permission of **Random House, Inc.** Electronic format use by permission of **John Hawkins & Associates, Inc.**

**UNDERSTANDING WHAT YOU READ** After you have finished reading the selection, answer the following questions in the space provided.

**1.** Give a brief history of Malcolm X's life.

_____

_____

**2.** What are some of the things that Malcolm X says people have said about him? What does he say about their charges?

_____

_____

**3.** Does Malcolm X say he is for violence? Explain your answer.

_____

_____

**4.** What does Malcolm X say is the only true way to achieve brotherhood between blacks and whites?

_____

_____

**5.** What advice does Malcolm X give to sincere white people?

_____

_____

HRW material copyrighted under notice appearing earlier in this work.

**6.** What do you think of Malcolm X's solution for bringing equality to African Americans in the 1960s? Explain your answer.

_____

_____

## ACTIVITY

Imagine that you are an activist in the 1960s who is preparing to march in a civil rights demonstration. Create a protest sign to carry to the demonstration that expresses your feelings about American racism or racial separation.

HRW material copyrighted under notice appearing earlier in this work.

**EPILOGUE**

## Modern America

★ ★ ★ ★ ★ ★ ★ ★ ★ ★ ★ ★ ★ ★ ★ ★ ★ ★ ★ ★ ★ ★ ★

# BIOGRAPHY READING

# Madeleine Albright

*Madeleine Albright has worked as a university professor, political adviser, and diplomat. In 1997 she became the first woman to serve as U.S. Secretary of State. As secretary of state, Albright promoted her belief that the United States should use its military and political power to fulfill its foreign policy goals.*

Madeleine Jana Korbel was born in 1937 in Prague, Czechoslovakia. The daughter of a Czech diplomat, she fled to England with her family when their country was invaded by Nazi Germany in 1939. (Some 40 years later she discovered that three of her grandparents had died in the Holocaust.) The Korbels returned to Prague after World War II, but when the Czech government fell to a communist coup in 1948, they were again forced to live abroad. The United States granted them political asylum, and by the end of 1949 they had settled in Colorado.

During the early 1950s, Korbel attended a small private school and became familiar with her new home country. She also became fluent in English, one of five languages that she now speaks. In 1955 Korbel entered Wellesley College, where she edited the school newspaper and studied political science. She graduated with honors four years later.

Three days after her graduation from college, Korbel married Joseph Albright, a journalist. A short time later she moved with her husband to New York, where in 1961 she gave birth to twin daughters. Over the next 10 years Madeleine Albright spent much of her time caring for her new family. She also went to graduate school at Columbia University, where she eventually earned a Ph.D. in Public Law and Government.

Albright's political career began in 1972, when she worked as a fundraiser for Edmund S. Muskie, a senator from Maine. She impressed Muskie with her knowledge of foreign policy, and in 1976 she became his chief legislative assistant in Washington. Two years later Albright joined the staff of President Jimmy Carter's National Security Council. By the end of the decade, she had earned a reputation as one of the Democratic Party's brightest members.

During the 1980s and early 1990s, Albright was a professor of international affairs at Georgetown University. She won four "teacher of the year" awards at Georgetown and directed the school's Women in Foreign Service Program. At the same time Albright remained active in the Democratic Party. After her divorce in 1983, she hosted a series of informal dinners that allowed party members to gather and talk strategy. She also served as a foreign-policy adviser to the party's presidential candidates in 1984, 1988, and 1992.

HRW material copyrighted under notice appearing earlier in this work.

Shortly after his election in 1992, President Bill Clinton chose Albright to serve as the U.S. delegate to the United Nations (UN). Only the second woman to fill that post, she soon became known at the UN as a skilled and aggressive diplomat. Among the issues she dealt with were ethnic conflicts in Eastern Europe and the actions of Iraq in the Middle East.

After four years as a delegate to the UN, Albright was nominated for secretary of state by President Clinton. The Senate confirmed her nomination unanimously, and in 1997 she became the highest-ranking woman in the U.S. government. During her first year on the job, Albright traveled to Africa, Asia, Europe, the Middle East, and Latin America to conduct foreign policy. She continues to promote U.S. interests around the world.

**UNDERSTANDING WHAT YOU READ**  After you have finished reading the selection, answer the following questions in the space provided.

**1.** Why did the Korbel family settle in the United States?

_____

_____

**2.** What did Madeleine Albright do during the 1960s?

_____

_____

**3.** When did Albright's political career begin?

_____

_____

**4.** How did Albright remain active in the Democratic Party during the 1980s and early 1990s?

_____

_____

**5.** Where did Albright travel to conduct foreign policy during her first year as secretary of state?

_____

_____

**ACTIVITY**

On a separate sheet of paper, write a letter to Madeleine Albright that asks a question about U.S. foreign policy.

HRW material copyrighted under notice appearing earlier in this work.

# ANSWER KEY

## Chapter 1

### PRIMARY SOURCE

1. lived on an island that floated in the air
2. because she was pregnant
3. duck, beaver, muskrat, turtle, water birds
4. The two brothers are described as opposites, one focused on creation and one on destruction.

### Activity

Students might draw the floating island or the animals that try to raise the *oeh-da*.

### LITERATURE

1. sound of the bugles; prepare for battle
2. The army would turn back.
3. effective literary device, helps to make them seem even more menacing, shows the Saracen army was rich and powerful, lets reader visualize the armies
4. Roland does not want to disgrace himself, his family's name, his king, or his country. The ideas contained in the code of chivalry center on bravery, loyalty to one's lord or king, honor, and duty.
5. Answers will vary. Students should understand how religion played an important role in the battles and other events during the Middle Ages.

### Activity

Students should accurately recount the story of the Battle of Roncevaux.

### BIOGRAPHY

1. to earn money to support her family
2. wrote about things she was familiar with, such as widowhood, courtly love, social criticism, and some philosophical issues; also wrote about the reality of women's lives in medieval France
3. believed that women should accept and fulfill roles as wives and mothers
4. French royal court and King Charles VI read her poetry; they could help fund Pisan's work and help establish and publicize her literary reputation

### Activity

Letters might mention that the French royal court and King Charles VI enjoyed de Pisan's poetry.

## Chapter 2

### PRIMARY SOURCE

1. thought he had reached the province of Cathay, or mainland China
2. The landscape was beautiful, with its mountains, many islands, and large variety of plants and animals.
3. that Columbus and his men had come from heaven
4. gold, spices, cotton, mastic and Indian slaves
5. because they were scarce or unknown in Spain

### Activity

Students' stamps should illustrate Columbus's arrival in the New World.

### LITERATURE

1. the elaborate and costly banquets held by the Great Khan, as well as the festivals held on the Great Khan's birthday and the new year
2. indicated the guests' place in the social order—the higher the person in the social hierarchy, the higher he would be seated; The Great Khan sat higher than any of his guests because he was the ruler of the society.
3. Expensive gifts would demonstrate the Great Khan's wealth and power and encourage loyalty.
4. Europeans rarely left the village or town they were born in; tales of distant lands and foreign cultures may have been of great interest

### Activity

Students' advice letters should include information on where the person should sit and how the person should behave at the table.

HRW material copyrighted under notice appearing earlier in this work.

## BIOGRAPHY

1. They were trying to reach fellow Spaniards in Mexico in order to return home to Spain.
2. as a healer and medicine man
3. Spaniards in Mexico wanted to enslave the Indians who had escorted him to Mexico.
4. served as governor of the Río de la Plata region of Brazil and then as a Spanish official in Africa

### Activity

Maps should include the path Cabeza de Vaca and his companions traveled as well as the major rivers, oceans, and seas.

## Chapter 3

### PRIMARY SOURCE

1. would provide the French with more information about the landscape, including rivers and mines; French would also learn more about the many Native American tribes in the area
2. If some accident were to happen to the young Frenchman, the French would declare war against the Algonquin.
3. to ensure that the Algonquin would treat the French boy well
4. The exchange would provide each group with more information about the other, and encourage understanding and friendly relations.

### Activity

Students should write five questions that they would ask the young Ochateguin.

### LITERATURE

1. describes a lot of the physical geography details, such as hills and ravines, as well as what he calls the "West Coast Sea" (Pacific Ocean)
2. certain topographical characteristics, such as abundance of water, vegetation, and whether or not the area would support farming; interested in establishing missions
3. Native Americans very accommodating to the Spaniards, treated them well, fed them, and provided them with shelter; may have been acquainted with the Spanish, or they may have thought they were sent by the gods

4. Native Americans conducted themselves like real businessmen and were shrewd in their trades.
5. Serra, who is a Franciscan missionary, probably wants to convert the Native Americans to Christianity.

### Activity

Students should create a sketch of the mission grounds with labels indicating the locations of important buildings.

## BIOGRAPHY

1. through faith
2. They resented the power and wealth of the church.
3. because of his heretical teachings and because Luther refused to go to Rome when summoned and burned the decree that the pope issued against him
4. All believers could have a direct relationship with God without the need for a priest.

### Activity

Students should prepare an outline about how they would go about reforming the church. They should also prepare a concise list of what the counterarguments might be.

## Chapter 4

### PRIMARY SOURCE

1. They meet to exchange letters.
2. guides were valuable because they knew the area, and Knight being a woman who was traveling alone, probably felt safer being accompanied by a man
3. roads were filled with rocks and mountainous passes

### Activity

Students might mention such items as water, food, and arrangement for a guide.

### LITERATURE

1. 12 colonists were killed, 24 captured
2. afraid of the weapons of the attackers and of dying
3. celebrate their victorious raid and have a feast using the animals they have captured
4. God carried her along and bore her spirit so that it did not fail.

HRW material copyrighted under notice appearing earlier in this work.

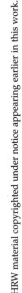

## Activity

Students' accounts might discuss working as slaves in the fields from sunup to sundown, while the villagers read and otherwise entertain themselves.

## BIOGRAPHY

1. in 1605; he was kidnapped and then sold as a slave in Spain
2. that his tribe had been killed, probably by smallpox
3. acted as a guide and interpreter, helped the Pilgrims to negotiate treaties with the Indians, showed the Pilgrims how to plant corn, and showed them where the best fishing spots were
4. because of his close relationship with the colonists and because he said he had the power to spread the plague

## Activity

Students should include the title of their movie, some significant scenes that they would include, and what the main theme of the movie would be.

# Chapter 5

## PRIMARY SOURCE

1. sinners being suspended above a great furnace of wrath by a slender thread held by the hand of God
2. Every soul that has not been born again is in danger of wrath and misery, even those who are very moral and religious.
3. by describing to his listeners the terrible fate awaiting those who are not saved and by pointing out how many people have recently come to Christ and how happy they are

## Activity

Students should create an advertisement that accurately conveys the same message as Jonathan Edwards's sermon.

## LITERATURE

1. crowded tightly together below deck, no fresh air and the stench of human waste and perspiration made many slaves ill, most in chains

2. While the ship was in port, but only until the ship began to make preparations to leave port; those who fell ill were allowed above deck to breathe fresh air.
3. When they were hungry, some tried to steal bits of fresh fish; others tried to jump overboard in an attempt to kill themselves.
4. The men treated them as if they were animals.

## Activity

Students' editorials should include specific arguments for why readers should oppose the slave trade.

## BIOGRAPHY

1. went to Quaker School during the winters and also taught himself literature, history, science, and math
2. after a traveling salesman gave him a pocket watch, which he took apart and reassembled
3. worked as a surveyor and reproduced the city plans from memory after the chief city planner stormed off with the plans
4. sunrises and sunsets, tides in the Chesapeake Bay, phases of the moon, recipes, medical remedies, and abolitionist essays
5. Answers will vary.

## Activity

Students' table of contents might contain such items as weather information, traffic, and the time the sun rises.

# Chapter 6

## PRIMARY SOURCE

1. local group of American Indians worked with the Virginia militia in this encounter; American Indians helped provide Washington with crucial information about the location of the French, and the Half King worked with Washington to plan and carry out an attack on the French
2. on a diplomatic mission, traveling as ambassadors to the Virginia capitol
3. instructions given to the French officers to investigate the area around the Potomac River
4. well; gave them the respect due imprisoned officers

HRW material copyrighted under notice appearing earlier in this work.

**5.** Washington captured and held French officers who officially had done nothing more than travel through the Appalachian Mountains. The French may have considered this capture an unprovoked act of war.

### Activity

Students' journal entries should describe the completed fort as well as their feelings about how it will help their military efforts.

### LITERATURE

1. of freedom or slavery
2. three million people are armed in the holy cause of liberty; the desire to be free
3. chains
4. retreating; going to war

### Activity

Students' posters or flyers should persuade people to support the Revolutionary War effort.

### BIOGRAPHY

1. plays, poems, and historical works
2. Both her husband and her brother were involved.
3. It gave the federal government too much power.
4. She knew about both the political events and personalities, and she analyzes the personal motives of individuals involved on both sides of the war.
5. the ability of women to be interested in more than merely domestic issues

### Activity

Students' bulletin boards should illustrate visually the major events in Warren's life as well as her opinions about politics and women's roles.

## Chapter 7

### PRIMARY SOURCE

1. 5,000; the ill are not getting better because the hospitals are so bad
2. diseases caught while in the hospital
3. to keep the men from going outside and from getting into fights
4. fresh air and wholesome food

### Activity

Students' letters should include the horrible conditions in the hospitals.

### LITERATURE

1. that people must be willing to fight or lose their freedom
2. uses an emotional appeal
3. people who are only willing to serve when it is easy
4. to help make his point
5. they will become slaves

### Activity

Students' book jackets should capture the main idea of the book and the reason it was written.

### BIOGRAPHY

1. engraving portraits, making bookplates, writing political cartoons
2. helped organize it and was one of the men who dressed up as a Mohawk Indian and threw tea overboard
3. to warn patriots to move their military supplies from the town
4. designing and printing the first issue of Continental currency, learning and supervising the process of manufacturing gunpowder, and making the first official seal for the colonies
5. disobedience, unsoldierly conduct, and cowardice

### Activity

Students should draw a scene or sketch one of the events of Paul Revere's life and write a descriptive caption to accompany it.

## Chapter 8

### PRIMARY SOURCE

1. the Seneca Lords, and if they agree with the Mohawk council, then it goes to the Cayuga and Oneida
2. carefully considered and then voted upon; "Added to the Rafter"
3. must not be quick to anger, take offensive action, or criticize; hearts should be full of good will and their minds should be focused on the welfare of their people

HRW material copyrighted under notice appearing earlier in this work.

★ ★ ★ ★ ★ ★ ★ ★ ★ ★ ★ ★ ★ ★ ★ ★ ★ ★ ★ ★ ★ ★ ★ ★ ★ ★ ★ ★ ★ ★

## Activity

Pro—The tribes could be more powerful together. Con—The tribes might want to maintain their autonomy.

## LITERATURE

1. accomplishments of the American colonists, including establishing good settlements, taming the wilderness, and innovations in the arts and sciences
2. no aristocratic class in America, no royal courts, no kings, no bishops or other church powers, no great manufacturers, no excessive luxuries; rich and poor are not very separated
3. did not have a chance to succeed in Europe; because of religious factionalism and persecution, some because of misery and want, some because of general restlessness
4. A man comes to America where he receives ample rewards for labors; the rewards allow a man to buy property; and property ensures that they are freemen. The laws of America help to ensure this process.

## Activity

Students' entries should include information about important events in Crèvecoeur's life.

## BIOGRAPHY

1. served as a trustee of Alexandria and a justice of the Fairfax County court
2. thought of ways the colonists could avoid paying the Stamp Act, Townsend duties, and other economically crushing laws that Britain had imposed on the American colonists
3. Virginia's Declaration of Rights, the Virginia constitution, the U.S. Constitution and the Bill of Rights
4. because he had insisted on the inclusion of a bill of rights

## Activity

Students' questions and answers should adequately explore Mason's life and his involvement with the creation of the U.S. Constitution.

## Chapter 9

## PRIMARY SOURCE

1. the "necessary and proper" clause in Section 8 of Article I
2. No, he thinks that it will be one central government.
3. Individual states will eventually be done away with by the growing power of the federal government.
4. laying and collecting taxes; regulating trade, raising and supporting armies, organizing, arming and disciplining the militia, instituting courts, and other general powers
5. Those vested with power usually increase it and remove everything that stands in their way.

## Activity

Students' cartoons or comic strips should explain what they think would happen to state governments under a new federal system according to the author's prediction in the reading.

## LITERATURE

1. willingness to do one's duty, hatred of corruption, greed, and tyranny; love of justice
2. The rest of the world is watching America to see if democracy and self-rule can succeed.
3. will wreck the hopes of others who look to America with the hope that the republic will succeed in bringing liberty and justice to all of its citizens
4. their duty toward their neighbors, family, and nation
5. Good civic education of the average citizen was very important to Roosevelt. Without it, he believed that the nation itself would encounter disaster and misfortune.

## Activity

Students' reviews should give both positive and negative reactions to Roosevelt's *The Free Citizen*.

## BIOGRAPHY

1. the American Revolution
2. to ask Spain for more money for the war effort and to get the Spanish government to recognize American independence; they

HRW material copyrighted under notice appearing earlier in this work.

would not recognize the United States but did provide money and weapons

3. that citizens of one state had the right to sue another state; to protect states from being sued

4. became the governor of New York

### Activity

Students' eulogies should include information about John Jay's life and his contributions to the United States.

## Chapter 10

### PRIMARY SOURCE

1. to evade bondage of system and habit, of family maxims, class opinions, and national prejudices; accept tradition only as means of information, use facts only as a way to do something different or better, and to seek the reasons of things for oneself

2. Each American appeals only to the individual effort of his own understanding.

3. believe that everything in the world may be explained, that nothing is beyond understanding, they deny what they cannot comprehend, and they do not believe in what can be called extraordinary or supernatural

4. releases men to their own conduct and of opening before the mind of each one of them an almost limitless perspective

5. that people may not always agree or think the same way but they will cooperate to pursue common interests and goals

### Activity

Students' travel brochures should describe the unique characteristics of the citizens of the country they select.

### LITERATURE

1. Major Sanford; advice from her friends and from General Richman and his wife

2. because she worried her friends

3. No. Lucy still thinks that Eliza likes Major Sanford.

4. that he has vicious habits and abandoned character; she does not like him at all

### Activity

Students' letters might contain such suggestions as to ignore him or to speak to him briefly and then move on.

### BIOGRAPHY

1. shared in her brother's lessons as he prepared for Harvard; he continued to teach her when he was home from school

2. poetry and essays

3. began to write about better access to education for young women

4. religion, politics, education, social manners, and how girls should be raised

### Activity

Students' advice letters should include reasons why young women and girls should have access to an education.

## Chapter 11

### PRIMARY SOURCE

1. it allows for differences of opinion to be tolerated and decided by reason

2. wise and frugal, restrains people from injuring one another, lets people freely pursue industry and improvement, and does not take things away from the people who have earned them

3. equal and exact justice to all, despite status, political affiliations, or religious beliefs; freedom of religion; freedom of the press; freedom of the person; trial by juries

4. peace, commerce, and honest friendship with all nations, entangling alliances with none; support of the rights of state governments; maintaining a well-disciplined militia; economy in public expense; payment of debts; preservation of public faith; encouragement of agriculture and commerce; diffusion of information

### Activity

Students should list some of the topics they would cover and what they would say about the U.S. government and the Constitution if they were giving an inaugural address.

### LITERATURE

1. members of the Osage tribe

2. cheating, insulting, killing, and taking the land of the American Indians

3. Unless the Osages unite with the Shawnee, the white men will destroy the Shawnee, then the Osages, and then all the other Native American nations; the white men

HRW material copyrighted under notice appearing earlier in this work.

want to keep the tribes divided so they are easier to defeat.

**4.** He is their friend.

**5.** He is angry with them.

### Activity

Students should create a slogan that illustrates either support for or opposition to joining the Shawnee.

### BIOGRAPHY

1. Shoshone; near Lemhi, Idaho
2. acted as an interpreter and guide and helped to get aid for the expedition from Shoshone; she was never paid for her services for the expedition
3. One account has it that Sacagawea died of a bad fever when she was about 25 years old. The other account is that Sacagawea returned to live with her people and lived among them until she was 100 years old. Students should understand that many births and deaths during this time were not recorded.
4. a river, a mountain peak, a mountain pass, two statues, a boulder, a monument, a public fountain, and a cement shaft

### Activity

Students' designs should accurately reflect Sacagawea's contributions to U.S. history.

## Chapter 12

### PRIMARY SOURCE

1. Soldiers forced Cherokees from their homes and into stockades where they waited until the journey to the Indian Territory began.
2. on foot, by horseback, and in oxen-drawn wagons
3. clothes, utensils, wagons, oxen, and materials for shelter
4. Answers will vary. Supporters may have been concerned only with the money or may have known that it was inevitable the U.S. government would force them off their lands. Opponents probably did not want to leave their ancestral homes.

### Activity

Students' letters should include descriptions of their duties, the conditions of the journey, and some of the events that occurred along the Trail of Tears.

### LITERATURE

1. basically content but lazy man, somewhat idle, careless, and foolish
2. to get away from work and his wife; a very strange man with a keg who leads him to a group of strange men playing nine-pins
3. some of the beverage from the keg; it is the next morning
4. an old lady in the village recognizes Rip; 20 years
5. all the events leading up to and including the American Revolution

### Activity

Students' stories might include a description of how their town or city has changed, differences in people they once knew, events that have happened, or how technology has changed.

### BIOGRAPHY

1. as one of the leading "War Hawks," a group that favored war with Great Britain
2. protectionist tariffs that support home manufacturing, internal improvements such as roads and canals, and a national bank
3. refused to back the annexation of Texas
4. believed that no such right existed

### Activity

Students' proverbs might discuss the art of compromise or point to the wisdom of negotiating.

## Chapter 13

### PRIMARY SOURCE

1. thought it was fun
2. impressed at its size and power
3. made her windowseat into a small library of poetry, pasting its side all over with newspaper clippings; carried leaves from a torn Testament in her pocket
4. filled the mill with houseplants, kept themselves clean and neat

HRW material copyrighted under notice appearing earlier in this work.

### Activity

Students' letters might include such things as the long workday and cumbersome rules of the boardinghouses.

### LITERATURE

1. four o'clock in the morning; it is a bad time to be leaving
2. It is full of people sleeping everywhere.
3. by the noise; some yawn, some groan, nearly all spit, and a few get up
4. "All right!" reflects the British interest in correctness, while "Go ahead!" reflects the American emphasis on progress.

### Activity

Students' book covers could include Dickens's boarding on the ship, the men awakening, or the men watching him as he combs his hair with his own comb.

### BIOGRAPHY

1. drawing and mechanical objects
2. because they would be the foundation of industry and transportation and that economic and political expansion would depend on rivers and canals
3. it broke apart and sank because it was not strong enough to support its steam engines
4. August 17, 1807; Hudson River

### Activity

Students' paragraphs might discuss people's happiness as they watch the *Clermont* travel up the Hudson River.

## Chapter 14

### PRIMARY SOURCE

1. The price of cotton in New Orleans was very good, but he was worried about the current year's crop because of the heavy rain that year.
2. He had to accept corn instead of cash since no one had the cash to rent it.
3. He had heard that the land in North Carolina was no longer fertile, and he believed that Eaton might want to move to more productive land in Tennessee.
4. He believed that if Eaton sold Bartons Creek, he would not make back the amount of money spent on the improvements, or that if Eaton decided to move Bartons Creek,

he would not be pleased by improvements made by the current tenant.

### Activity

Students' letters might include information on renting land and growing crops.

### LITERATURE

1. in response to a nearby slave rebellion coordinated by a man named Nat Turner
2. saw it as a chance to exercise power, authority, and even fear over the African Americans of the community
3. Searchers planted evidence such as powder and shot to prove that the slaves were plotting insurrection, whipped slaves at random, and stole items from their homes.
4. The church was demolished.
5. to annoy the poor whites by showing that they lived in a comfortable and well-ordered house

### Activity

Students' paragraphs might explore the abuse of slaves and the inability of slaves to worship.

### BIOGRAPHY

1. She accepted the marriage proposal from Pierce Butler and was looking for a change of pace.
2. Her husband's family did not think that acting was an honorable profession, Kemble did not behave like an obedient southern wife, and she had abolitionist views.
3. to fight against the Confederate sympathies of her British friends
4. writing

### Activity

Students' murals might contain such events as Kemble acting in *Romeo and Juliet*, living on a southern plantation, or fighting her husband's family.

## Chapter 15

### PRIMARY SOURCE

1. They are the most wretched, degraded, and abject set of beings that have ever lived.
2. the assertion by some whites in America that African Americans are not fully human and that they descended from monkeys

HRW material copyrighted under notice appearing earlier in this work.

3. White Americans claim to be enlightened and Christian, yet they continue to treat slaves in a very un-Christian manner.
4. God; He deserves to be killed by his enemies.
5. Answers will vary, but students should recognize that the illustration is intended to describe the condition of African Americans as compared to white Americans, and African Americans have many more obstacles to overcome in achieving liberty.

### Activity

Students' pictures or political cartoons should illustrate the extreme differences in the way most black and white Americans lived at the time.

### LITERATURE

1. to attract the notice and win the attentions of men
2. because they have influence over the minds and character of children of both sexes
3. A woman who goes out to wash is not paid as much as a man even though the work she is doing is just as hard.
4. It would add strength and dignity to women's characters and teach them more true sympathy.

### Activity

Students' children's books should thoroughly explore the challenges that faced many women in the mid-1800s.

### BIOGRAPHY

1. She mastered English grammar in four days and Latin grammar in three days.
2. based on the subjects taught at Amherst College; added modern languages and music
3. by assigning each student a particular household task
4. that education was intellectual, physical, and spiritual and that a broad range of subjects helped to develop the individual

### Activity

Students' journal entries might include such tasks as cleaning or cooking, going to class, attending gym class, and studying.

## Chapter 16

### PRIMARY SOURCE

1. It was the first time such a large group of people had traveled west.
2. A large number of cattle could not survive on the scanty pasture available, nor could wagons be taken on so rugged and mountainous a route.
3. No progress could be made with so cumbersome and undisciplined a body.
4. They are brave for undertaking such a journey.

### Activity

Students might draw the large parties that traveled to Independence Rock or the smaller parties that traveled through the Rocky Mountains.

### LITERATURE

1. to bring a poet from New Mexico to compete with the Californian poet Gracia
2. They make him sit in a chair by the wall and do not invite him to eat with them.
3. tells them a story about a baby goat having to wait to be fed that makes the ranch owner realize that he is being rude

### Activity

Students' headlines should accurately reflect the content of the story.

### BIOGRAPHY

1. to fulfill his father's dream of starting an American colony in Texas
2. The Mexican government refused to recognize the Spanish land grant given to his father; he traveled to Mexico City where he pleaded his case before the new government.
3. would try to work out a compromise between the Americans and Mexican government
4. was not very successful in getting approval for a state government in Texas, and on his way back Mexican officials arrested him

### Activity

Students' letters might explore Austin's work to settle Texas and to maintain order between Americans and Mexicans.

HRW material copyrighted under notice appearing earlier in this work.

## Chapter 17

### PRIMARY SOURCE

1. that U.S. citizens are racially superior to the Mexicans
2. that slavery would exist in Texas regardless of its political status
3. opposed to the war; thought it was about stealing land from Mexico
4. slavery
5. that free states should leave the slave states alone; he also believed that the country should not prevent slavery from dying a natural death

### Activity

Students' plays should discuss reasons why some Americans opposed the Mexican War.

### LITERATURE

1. felt a bitter resentment against his people
2. retroactive laws
3. Mexicans and Americans were to have equal rights under the treaty.
4. gold rush
5. "The forbidden fruit is the sweetest"; that they just want the land of the Mexican people

### Activity

Students' paragraphs should mention that the treaty guaranteed that the Mexican people would retain ownership of their land.

### BIOGRAPHY

1. read the *Book of Mormon* by Joseph Smith and became a convert to the religion
2. Young was first a successful Mormon missionary, then was appointed to the Quorum of the Twelve Apostles, and then became the leading financial officer of the church. When Joseph Smith was killed in 1844, Young assumed leadership of the church.
3. Many people did not agree with the church's views or practices.
4. Some historians think that Young might have thought that the geography would prevent other settlers from moving into the area. He hoped that the physical isolation would strengthen the bond between the church and the community.

### Activity

Students' maps should show the movement of the Mormons from western New York to Illinois to Utah.

## Chapter 18

### PRIMARY SOURCE

1. the devil and his fallen angels
2. "Give me Liberty or give me Death"
3. because they do not allow black Americans to defend their liberty and freedom the same way that white American revolutionaries defended theirs
4. to demand a repeal of the Fugitive Slave Act; to rise up and defend themselves against tyranny, even if it means death

### Activity

Students' letters might discuss the fact that African American slaves were human beings who were guaranteed the same rights as whites.

### LITERATURE

1. Slaves were property and had to be evaluated with the rest of the estate.
2. horses, sheep, and swine for inspection
3. could mean that husbands and wives, families, and close friends could be sent to different places
4. Douglass was given to Mrs. Lucretia as opposed to Master Andrew, who was a cruel and vicious master.
5. Answers will vary, but students should realize that the brutality inflicted on slaves was being treated as something less than human, but that the brutality that slave owners suffered was having to be callous and mean enough to treat them as less than human.

### Activity

Students' murals might contain such items as Douglass's work to learn to read, his escape from slavery, the publication of his autobiography, or his work in the abolition movement.

### BIOGRAPHY

1. the "War Hawks," a group of young men who wanted war against Great Britain
2. praised slaveholding and warned the North of the dangers of southern desperation

HRW material copyrighted under notice appearing earlier in this work.

★ ★ ★ ★ ★ ★ ★ ★ ★ ★ ★ ★ ★ ★ ★ ★ ★ ★ ★ ★ ★ ★ ★ ★ ★ ★ ★ ★ ★ ★

3. any law was immediately null and void if the people of any state thought it unconstitutional

4. that the North would abolish slavery, that the North and South would fight, and that Northern whites and freed slaves would unite to subjugate southern whites

## Activity

Students might mention Calhoun's work to keep the slave system intact.

# Chapter 19

## PRIMARY SOURCE

1. to see if there are any possessions left in their house in Baton Rouge; because she had a dream the night before that a lot of their possessions had been saved in trunks

2. that she said she would marry a Federal officer if she loved him

3. convicts set free; slaves and Yankee soldiers looting the abandoned houses and stealing jewelry from women

4. helps the servants fill up their canteens with water; soldiers are incredibly thankful that a lady is helping them

5. Talking to soldiers was one of the best ways for women to gather information about their families and where they needed to go for safety.

## Activity

Students' museum exhibits should be both creative and informative and should include information about military and civilian life in the North and the South.

## LITERATURE

1. 1-1/2 miles; a large group of injured men with very little shelter

2. His wound is not very serious and he wants the doctors to treat men who are more severely wounded first.

3. He administers chloroform to himself to ease the pain.

4. Answers will vary, but students should understand that medical care was not very advanced and that a lot of wounded men died.

5. Students' selections will vary, but the passage they select should be descriptive or realistic in nature.

## Activity

Students' letters should describe what happened to them after they were wounded, the kind of treatment they received, and events that occurred around them.

## BIOGRAPHY

1. Some men had a difficult time working with a woman and dealing with her success.

2. organized efforts to get badly needed food, supplies, and medical equipment to soldiers on the battlefield; "Angel of the Battlefield"

3. She organized the American Red Cross.

4. during times of war, droughts, floods, outbreaks of yellow fever, railway accidents, and other domestic disasters

## Activity

Students' questions and answers should accurately reflect the life and work of Clara Barton.

# Chapter 20

## PRIMARY SOURCE

1. the Thirteenth and Fourteenth Amendments

2. that it does not have a tendency to destroy the legal equality of the two races or to re-establish slavery

3. to enforce the equality of the two races before the law; to enforce social equality, distinctions based on color, or a forced commingling of the races

4. the assumption that the enforced separation of the two races stamps the colored race with a badge of inferiority

5. almost 60 years

## Activity

Students' pictures should accurately reflect Homer Plessy's arrest on the railroad car, and their caption should point out how "separate-but-equal" treatment was unfair.

## LITERATURE

1. railroad passenger cars that were designated for African Americans to ride in

2. that separate cars and treatment received in those cars were a way of making African Americans feel inferior; being at the mercy

HRW material copyrighted under notice appearing earlier in this work.

of drunk white men, getting bad accommodations for first-class prices, and being subjected to swearing and cigar smoke

3. usually left the car and let the white men do as they pleased
4. The African American was usually arrested and was sometimes lynched, whipped, or tortured.
5. Answers will vary, but students should get the impression that the author is opposed to the concept of "separate yet equal" and believes that only the whites benefit by legal segregation.

### Activity

Students' editorials should describe the troubles they experienced on a "separate but equal" railroad car and explain what should be done to change the situation.

### BIOGRAPHY

1. moved around the Midwest where he attended various grade schools and worked at odd jobs to support himself; later attended Simpson College and Iowa State Agricultural College
2. piano and art; wanted to study agriculture full-time
3. taught classes, conducted research, supervised an experimental farm, published bulletins offering advice to farmers, established a "movable school of agriculture"
4. because they are high in protein and restore nitrogen to the soil
5. a fund for agricultural research at Tuskegee

### Activity

Students might mention Carver's persistence in getting an education, his work and teachings at the Tuskegee Institute, and his development of more than 300 uses for peanuts.

## Chapter 21

### PRIMARY SOURCE

1. usually 23 or 24 years old
2. stampedes, bad weather and storms, rough trails, cattle rustlers, headstrong or stranded cattle, dangers from riding in the middle of the night
3. The custom started after a cowboy and his horse were trampled in a stampede. The

singing was done so that the cowboys could know each other's locations in a stampede situation.

4. would follow the herd from a distance so they would not be noticed, then wait for a dark and rainy night and would wave a blanket to excite the cattle and then would lead them away from the cowhands
5. Students might mention the physical strain, the unpredictable weather, and dangers from rustlers and thieves; some of the rewarding aspects may include bringing the herd in on time, saving a stranded cow or saving a cow from a wild animal, or helping calves to be born.

### Activity

Students' movie posters might include such things as the cowhand, a stampede, or life in a cattle town.

### LITERATURE

1. to strike it rich
2. farming and ranching
3. cooking for the men, feeding the cattle at night, doctoring both the men and cattle, delivering babies, washing clothes
4. says that her mother felt it a disgrace to have begged in Pueblo

### Activity

Students' want ads might include information about striking it rich with little work.

### BIOGRAPHY

1. the Paiutes near Humboldt Lake, Nevada
2. because many of the parents did not want an American Indian girl to attend the school with their children; that her tribe had been moved to a reservation
3. worked as an interpreter; reported bad conduct, gave speeches, wrote a book about the conditions, and met with the president and the secretary of the interior
4. Answers will vary but students might answer that Winnemucca's efforts were important because people eventually started helping American Indians.

### Activity

Students' letters should include information about what the federal government can do to bring immediate help to the Paiute.

HRW material copyrighted under notice appearing earlier in this work.

# Epilogue

## PRIMARY SOURCE

1. did not transform one chemical element into another and produce radium, but merely separated it chemically from the mineral containing it; God
2. H. G. Wells; in 1933
3. If Szilard and his colleagues had discovered artificial radioactivity in the 1930s, it would have changed history and World War II very dramatically; their not discovering it led to peace.
4. Germans would have gotten hold of the nuclear fission technology and used it to win World War II in a matter of a few weeks after it began.
5. Students should recognize that Szilard has some reservations about the future uses of nuclear power, and his reference to the Devil may indicate his worry that the technology will be used for destructive purposes.

### Activity

Students' predictions should discuss both the benefits and the dangers of the discovery or invention.

## LITERATURE

1. born in Omaha, Nebraska, in 1925; in 1946 was imprisoned for robbery; in prison read about and studied the condition of African Americans, converted to the Black Muslim faith, and changed his name to Malcolm X; later became a minister in the Nation of Islam
2. "the angriest Negro in America" and "a teacher, a fomenter of violence;" said that he would not deny being the angriest Negro in America and that it is a lie that he is a fomenter of violence—he is for justice
3. says that he is for violence if non-violence means that African Americans will continue to be treated unfairly in America
4. through religion
5. to teach non-violence to other white people
6. Students should state their position and defend it with evidence.

### Activity

Students' protest signs will vary as to content, but they should include their feelings about American racism or the idea of racial separation.

## BIOGRAPHY

1. When the Czech government fell to a communist coup in 1948 they were forced to live abroad. The United States granted them political asylum.
2. spent much of her time caring for her new family; also went to graduate school at Columbia University, where she eventually earned a Ph.D. in Public Law and Government
3. in 1972 when she worked as a fund-raiser for Edmund S. Muskie, a senator from Maine
4. hosted a series of informal dinners that allowed party members to gather and talk strategy; also served as a foreign policy adviser to the party's presidential candidates in 1984, 1988, and 1992
5. Africa, Asia, Europe, the Middle East, and Latin America

### Activity

Students' letters should ask appropriate and thoughtful questions about current foreign policy issues.

HRW material copyrighted under notice appearing earlier in this work.